# Roots of Gratitude

· · · · · · ·

## A Young Man's Global Search
## for Happiness

DARIA HOSSEINYOUN

**TURNING
STONE
PRESS**

First published in 2013 by
Turning Stone Press, an imprint of
Red Wheel/Weiser, LLC
With offices at:
665 Third Street, Suite 400
San Francisco, CA 94107
*www.redwheelweiser.com*

ISBN: 978-1-61852-072-2

Cover design by Jim Warner
Cover image: Daria Hosseinyoun

Printed in the United States of America

10 9 8 7 6 5 4 3 2 1

*To my mother, for understanding, and my father, for supporting. I also want to dedicate this to my late friend, Will, who provided me the courage and perspective on life that it took to take this trip.*

# Contents

Acknowledgments     vii

Prologue     ix

Part One: Mongolia: The Test of Patience     1

    Chapter One     2

    Chapter Two     7

    Chapter Three     8

    Chapter Four     12

    Chapter Five     20

    Chapter Six     27

    Chapter Seven     33

    Chapter Eight     35

Part Two: Bali: Interlude in Paradise     43

    Chapter Nine     44

    Chapter Ten     49

    Chapter Eleven     51

Part Three: Japan: Grace in Discipline     67

    Chapter Twelve     68

    Chapter Thirteen     79

    Chapter Fourteen     87

    Chapter Fifteen     88

    Chapter Sixteen     91

    Chapter Seventeen     95

    Chapter Eighteen     103

Part Four: India: Challenges of Enlightenment          119
  Chapter Nineteen                                     120
  Chapter Twenty                                       133
  Chapter Twenty-One                                   140
  Chapter Twenty-Two                                   145
  Chapter Twenty-Three                                 152
  Chapter Twenty-Four                                  158
  Chapter Twenty-Five                                  174
  Chapter Twenty-Six                                   178
  Chapter Twenty-Seven                                 181

Part Five: Nepal: Gratitude in Unexpected Places       185
  Chapter Twenty-Eight                                 186
  Chapter Twenty-Nine                                  189
  Chapter Thirty                                       193
  Chapter Thirty-One                                   198
  Chapter Thirty-Two                                   200
  Chapter Thirty-Three                                 205
  Chapter Thirty-Four                                  207
  Chapter Thirty-Five                                  214
  Chapter Thirty-Six                                   222

Part Six: Everest: Roots of Gratitude                  235
  Chapter Thirty-Seven                                 236
  Chapter Thirty-Eight                                 244
  Chapter Thirty-Nine                                  246
  Chapter Forty                                        249
  Chapter Forty-One                                    253

Epilogue                                               259

# Acknowledgments

I'd like to thank Mr. Steve Henrikson, for lighting up my path and watering the seed of my potential.

# Prologue

"Wake up! It's 7:00 AM!"

My father, wearing his workout clothes, barked out the order like a platoon sergeant at morning reverie. He was ready to tackle the gym.

Rolling out of bed, my eyes still heavy with sleep, I rustled around for any work-appropriate clothes I could find at this ungodly hour. A collared shirt and a pair of slacks were the best I could manage. To save time, I left without breakfast. I unlocked my new M3 for the drive to work.

At the office, my father's partner had coffee waiting for me.

"Hello, good man!" This was the nickname he gave me—I hope, by no coincidence.

It was our morning ritual to drink coffee and jaw about politics, girls, memories, and, most importantly, about how we believed life should be lived.

"If I could, I would go to Spain and play guitar for the rest of my life, like I did when I lived there in ninety-two!" he said.

The dream seemed so distant, as if travel to another galaxy in our lifetime would be for all practical purposes impossible. He had long ago given up on this dream, letting it become a quixotic musing.

At that moment, my dream seemed just as far away.

"I would like to go to Nepal and live in a monastery. I would like to reach a state of ultimate happiness," I said.

He chuckled more about how both of us were right about how to live our lives. Certainly, neither of us had been living them.

After coffee we continued with our hectic day, answering incessant complaint calls, running back and forth from property to property, going through the ever-growing stack of tenant requests, and managing vendors as they sloppily worked around the property. We inevitably became the next victims for angry tenants, without even a moment to think twice about the conversation we just had. As we wound ourselves tighter in the daily routine, our stress levels rose.

I went through the seemingly insurmountable mountain of tenant complaints that covered my desk and before I could even begin to confront the pile, the phone rang.

"Our roof is leaking and we are holding you responsible!"

*Me? Did I put a hole in their roof? Did I sabotage their roof intentionally?* I sure felt like I did after that conversation.

I got through the rest of the workday only to feel drained at the end of it. Before leaving the office, I made an energy drink strong enough to handle the gym routine. As I mindlessly mixed this enigmatic red powder into water and stirred, I wondered what kind of crap I was about to put in my body. I climbed into my white supercharged BMW again (the most exciting part of my day), heading to the sports club with my gear, a pair of basketball shorts, and a breathable white Nike t-shirt. I felt a surreal sense of energy, like I had just slept for twelve hours and slammed down three coffees and three shots of vodka as a chaser.

At the gym, the same dull routine played out: Bench press, dumbbell press, incline, decline . . . Repeat. Another sacrifice I was making in my day in order not to lose my muscle. Desperate to break up the ennui of this regimen, I scanned the gym, hoping to find someone I knew. No luck. Just other zombies who had given themselves over to this numbing existence for ten, twenty, thirty, or even forty years running.

In the locker room, it was hard not to eavesdrop.

"How you doing, Joe?"

"Well, I'm surviving this economy."

"I know, it's really looking bad, did you hear about Fannie Mae?"

"Yeah, I think it will get worse."

It sickened me to hear this regurgitation of the news, without exaggeration, for the tenth time in a week. The media's scare tactics had struck panic even in those who weren't actually affected. Take Joe. He'd just bought himself a new $200,000 Aston Martin. That hardly qualified as "surviving."

I jumped in the steam room to unwind and, after five minutes, my eyes focused on the clock outside: it was 7:00 PM. I ran out of the steam room, straight for the shower. As usual, I was late to meet my girlfriend for dinner.

"Hey, I think I'm gonna be a little late," I said as soon as she answered her cell phone.

"I know, I'm used to it. I know you too well."

I guess I wasn't efficient enough.

After driving for twenty minutes, I made it to the city, my girlfriend hopped in, and we were off to eat. Her face mirrored the signs of exhaustion, frustration, and futility in mine. However, at twenty-three, she found it easy to be optimistic and untainted, shielded from the inevitable fear of disappointment.

"Hey, baby! Are you hungry?" she asked.

"I'm starving! Where do you want to eat?"

"Let's go wherever you want!"

"Okay, how about some nice Persian food?"

"I know this nice Thai restaurant on Union everyone at work has been talking about. My sister says we got to go there. Yelp has given it four stars."

"Okay," I said with a hint of disappointment.

*Why do women even bother asking if they know exactly what they want?*

At the romantic and cozy restaurant, we ordered a glass of pinot noir and I was already thinking about ordering another when, as if on cue, my eyes stumbled upon the time. Eight forty-five. We had our food rushed to us and devoured it in minutes, not even stopping to decide if it was hitting the right tastebuds—that exhilarating sense of umami one would expect at a place like this.

"Dessert?" my girlfriend suggested.

"Well, it's nine-thirty and I'm kind of tired . . . " I said listlessly.

"Yeah, me too. Let's go home."

We went straight to bed, made semi-passionate and semi-exhausted love, and quickly fell asleep.

*Is this what my life will be like until retirement?*

I was fed up and hadn't even started down that long path yet. And apparently, I had it better than most . . .

∾

"Wake up! It's 7:00 AM!" my friend said in an urgent voice.

I rolled out of my sleeping bag, put my thermal pants on, and climbed outside the tent to see three towering camels outside, waiting for us. We were in the middle of the Gobi, Asia's largest desert—the world's fifth largest, where the land stretches for hundreds and hundreds of miles in every direction. The land is barren in this cold desert: pebbles and dirt can be seen for seemingly endless miles. Indeed, this was what it meant to be in the middle of nowhere. No matter how far you walked in any direction, you got to the same place you were before. Nowhere.

We were in the most remote part of the Gobi: a four-hour train ride north of China, away from any trace of modern society. We had spent the last five days in solitude, staying in a *ger*, exploring the inner labyrinths of our minds that had been stubbornly conditioned toward urgent daily schedules. We had no plans and absolutely nothing to do—all we could think to do was relax and enjoy being.

Upon our arrival in this vast expanse, the initial sense was exhilarating. However, only after a couple of hours, I already was anxious and nervous.

*How am I going to do nothing in the middle of nowhere for eight days?* This day, we traveled to the famous *lama* of the Gobi's monastery to see the *nadam* or festival. The tall camels lowered themselves gently so we could hop aboard and move forward in our modest caravan. The camels appeared preternaturally happy and serene as they marched steadily through the harsh conditions of the desert. Our pack was filled with *airag* (fermented horse's milk), breadsticks, and toilet paper.

My mind switched from a silent void mode and began to race through the reflections of my life back home in the U.S. and all of the zombies I would have been encountering now. Even here, in the world's most utterly unforgiving landscape, I could escape the 21st century realities of my conditioned mind. I was constantly refocusing.

After three hours of uneventful riding, I had a sore ass. We arrived at our destination.

"Let's eat and take a nap," my Mongolian friend suggested in his characteristic carefree tone, his worries limited to nothing more than when he would eat next as he sat atop cloud nine.

"It's only eleven-thirty in the morning. We just woke up a few hours ago."

"So?! I'm tired."

I looked around and it seemed like there was not much else on the agenda anyway. We certainly were not pressed for time, and the invitation to nap sounded strangely liberating.

Our Mongolian guide, who had taken time off from his cattle and farm to take us around, directed us to a floor in a shack and we fell asleep quickly. Two hours later, I woke up with the guide's terribly rotten teeth uncommonly close to my face. He spoke in Mongolian, his quick, excited, familiar rhythm sounding as if he was conversing with a native speaker. I didn't understand a word, but I had become accustomed to not knowing what was going on, and respected the value of communicating feelings by physical movement and gestures rather than words. Somehow, through our awkward charades, I discovered that he wanted me to see a horse race. So we hopped on our camels again for another thirty minutes and rushed to the race, only in time to see them finish.

Hundreds of horses could be seen in the distance and, as we neared the venue, we saw the riders were all children under seven, covering a fraction of the bony and lean racehorses they galloped on through the barren land. Later I found out that because of their small weight, the children make ideal jockeys. They raced fearlessly, with conviction burning in their eyes; their determination was downright scary. Not only were they prepared to compete, but they were prepared to win. The race ended abruptly and the crowd of cars and people disappeared. Apparently, they were off to see a local wrestling match. Arriving at what they call the energy circle of the Gobi, a twenty-minute camel ride from the horse race, we saw a crowd huddled as the local wrestling team challenged anyone who dared step up. One after another, people were pinned in the dirt and applause and laughter broke out. For a fleeting second, I felt like a spectator at a gladiator battle taking in the grand gestures, poses, and celebrations the wrestlers, dressed in traditional costumes, displayed. Their bright red Speedo-like shorts accentuated their massive calves as they set their heavy boots into the ground, ready to face the next opponent. They wore belts around their waists, which they used as leverage over their opponents.

"Let's go," I said to my friend after a half hour.

We walked over to a battered silver pickup truck from the 1970s and waited to be driven home. Finally, three hours later, the driver showed up drunk. Without saying a word, he rubbed two wires together to turn on the car— exactly like in the movies when thieves are stealing a vehicle. We cruised through the desert and the car nearly sputtered out several times along the way. Hardly surprisingly, the windows did not operate properly and they were stuck in the completely open position. The sun-warmed air of the day gave rapidly away to the pre-twilight chill. Our driver boisterously jabbered at us in Mongolian, his laugh revealing that half his teeth were missing.

When we made it back, we discovered that our tent had folded on itself and that all of our belongings that

had been provisioned for the entire week had accumulated a gritty layer from a dust storm. We quickly tried to
salvage what we could before sundown as the wind pelted
our faces, making it that much more difficult to move the
tent to a safer spot. We sat inside and ate our modest meal
in darkness. All night, the wind continued to threaten
the tent's stability and dust enveloped us, easily finding
our eyes, ears, and mouths.

A car's idling engine woke us from our fitful sleep. I
heard the van door slide open and female voices emerged.
I quickly calculated that three young French women were
staying in the ger next to our tent in the middle of nowhere.

~

# PART ONE

*Mongolia: The Test of Patience*

~

$$\backsim 1 \backsim$$

*This is my unedited story. I am not an angel, nor do I intend to be. I wish not to mask the truth but rather to give you the unscripted account of who I am. I carry the same needs and thoughts as any typical guy my age, but beneath is a depth that punches through the surface, always yearning for more. The material and immaterial sides show throughout this story. I believe it is healthy to have profoundly felt spiritual inclinations mixed in with the urge to give into worldly temptations. If you enjoy it, do it. Did I mention I'm a Gemini?*

It started in high school with my inability to accept God as it had been presented to me—as a perfect, all-knowing, all-powerful presence—throughout my formative years. If this indeed were the case, why then were so many people suffering all over the world? For me, the acknowledgment of this type of God demanded an explanation of why the existence of suffering was at total odds with "His" redeeming, rehabilitative traits.

As I began questioning, teachers began finding me. A particular teacher, Mr. Henrikson—a practicing Buddhist, at my high school—approached me during a debate I was having with a few counselors who happened to be fundamentalist Catholics. He sat in silence and listened to our debate, only interjecting when the others were not actually listening to my questions.

"Is God all-knowing and loves all things on the earth?" I said.

"Yes."

"Then how could He allow so many to suffer needlessly? What have they done to deserve to suffer? Kids in Africa, the Middle East, all over the world are suffering as this God watches? Why? Why would this kind of God create a world where suffering even exists?"

The counselors grew angry and impatient while Mr. Henrikson sat across the table with a gleam in his eye. I knew we were on the same page. His subtle smile confirmed that he understood me.

I knew this graceful old teacher possessed the wisdom I sought. His calmness and the time he took to respond to questions displayed his patience and genuine care for what we spoke about. I started meeting him weekly for discussions. We would speak for hours as he introduced me to the concepts of Buddhism. It was a fresh approach that I admired almost instantaneously. "Life is suffering" is how it began. As we went through my questions and tried to answer some of the most difficult ones, my soul was finally at ease, and I knew I was at the right place. Soon thereafter, I vowed to visit Nepal so I could learn from and meditate with the monks.

Four years passed as college and Los Angeles' superficialities sidetracked me. Lost in the huge metroplex crowd, I became increasingly more miserable as I looked at the world around me and the priorities that had manifested themselves into an uncompromising dog-eat-dog world of emptiness. In my twenties, I somehow remarkably had lost my own vision and priorities.

There was one friend, however, who maintained integrity through his every action: Will. He managed to be the perfect guy: a four-point-zero GPA throughout college, tall and handsome appearance, and a model of perfect individualism. Guys wanted to be him, and girls wanted to be with him, but no matter what, he never gave in to temptation. He knew exactly what he wanted and consistently went for it.

After several uncharacteristic anxiety attacks during his sophomore year of college, he went to a doctor who diagnosed him with a brain tumor. I watched as one of my best friends deteriorated in front of me. It was my first encounter with death's haunting face and a dreadful premature realization of my own vulnerability. I was wasting my life. I could have easily been in Will's place and, therefore, my days could have easily been numbered, like his.

Every night, my tears barricaded against the chance for a decent night's sleep. In hopes of knowing how to cope with the permanence of his absence, I waited for a message. Will's death shook me to my core and forced me to reassess my life. It's one thing to realize how precious life is. It's another to do something about it. I had the power to ensure that Will did not die in vain and that the lessons of his abbreviated life would become even clearer in his absence. He had died for a purpose; his death was a sacrifice for inspiration that could not be quieted. I had to pursue that passion for myself and for Will. Remembering my high school vow to go to Nepal, I regained that old sense of momentum.

With rejuvenated desire, I only had one last hurdle to overcome: fear. Why would anyone in their right mind want to get up and leave all the comforts of a luxurious life of five-star hotels, personal villas, and turbocharged cars to expose themselves to Third World lifestyles, and do it all alone? This essential step required more guts than I had at the time. However, gradually, people I hadn't spoken to in years reappeared in my life and told me the things I needed to hear.

"Do you believe in the universe and its powers?" my dad's accountant asked me. This man, in his early fifties, had a sparkle in his blue eyes and a smile that resonated in my heart. There was nothing but kindness in his eyes. He was the most spiritual person my father knew. He had written spiritual guidebooks and would speak of things I had never heard about before such as past lives, spiritual guides, and aliens and their roles on the earth.

"Yes."

"Do you believe that it has protected you and given you all that you need thus far?"

"Yes."

"Well, shouldn't you believe that it will continue to do so throughout your life?"

"I guess so."

"Don't settle down here yet. Go off and explore the world. There are so many wonderful things out there for you to experience and it will be something you will never regret your whole life. You've got plenty of time to make tons of money."

He handed me a pile of books on varying philosophies ranging from the *chakra* system to the history of aliens and their intervention in our world. As I read the pile of books over the next month, my courage strengthened; every word fortified my resolve to do what needed to be done.

∽

"Mom, Dad. I've decided I'm going to travel for a year."

There was an awkward protracted silence at the dinner table as my mom realized she had to face the music. I could see that she had to hide her fears in order to allow me to live my dream. She did the best she could not to reveal her desire to hold on.

"Why do you want to go?" she pleaded with me.

"It's just something I have to do."

"Where do you want to go?"

"I'm going to start in Mongolia to visit my friend. Then I'll go to Japan, India, and Nepal."

I might as well have said I wanted to go to Afghanistan because as far as they were concerned, these countries were going to be just as dangerous.

"When do you want to leave?"

"In two months." And, like that, it was set. I had committed myself and there was no turning back.

## ≈ 2 ≈

August 3, 2009. It all led to this day, this moment where I chose to leave it all behind—a girlfriend, family, two homes (one of which was like a personal Playboy mansion), the car of my dreams, and my comfortable job managing my family's properties. All would be abandoned to pursue a dream I had at the age of sixteen. That was six years ago.

I certainly left little doubt about my resolve. I canceled my cell phone service as I officially disconnected myself from everything I have ever known (other than my close family and friends). I had always wanted to delete all those numbers I never called and the people I hadn't seen or talked to for years. I had held on to what was no longer there. My life had been based on trying to hold on and preserve. I always thought I would be scared, nervous, and lost on my own. But, for the first time, I was completely peaceful, confident, and grounded.

I was hoping to get away from this materialism to find what lies beneath the superficiality. My goal, simply: truth. For this challenge, I did not have a mother or father. I had been sent to this world for a purpose. My success rested upon understanding this fact. I would not allow discomfort to bring me back. I could not return until I received what I needed in this world. The hardest part was taking the plunge; the rest was freefall.

The journey to Mongolia took about twenty-two hours from the minute I left my house and when I called home, my mother's voice already sounded distant. Though it had barely been one day, we were speaking like it had already been months.

On the plane from Seoul to Ulaanbaatar, I sat next to an American man and we started chatting.

"So, what you got going on in Mongolia?" I asked him.

"My wife is Mongolian and I'm here to take her son back to America with me."

"Wow, so, have you met the son before?"

"No, I have never met her family either, and I can't speak a word of Mongolian. I'm about to meet everyone, including my new son-in-law."

It was interesting to think that the two of us were going to the same remote country with two completely different perspectives and goals. He seemed nervous about his journey.

"What are you doing here?" he asked.

"I'm traveling around the world."

"How long have you been traveling?"

With that question, my heart dropped, thinking about just how young my journey still was—I had so little experience under my belt and such a long road ahead of me.

"This is my first stop." I managed to stammer.

I arrived at the airport where John, a Mongolian friend from Germany, was waiting to pick me up. He had just received his license and was eager to show off his driving skills. He loaded my stuff into his "new" car: a white 1990 Mitsubishi Pajero.

I was shocked to see the nearly deserted condition of Ulaanbaatar, Mongolia's capital. It looked as if this city were run by villagers and unmotivated businessmen. Even with just a little rain, the roads were flooded. Hotels were perched not on the main thoroughfare but behind other buildings and through flooded parking lots. I wondered how small cars maneuvered around town.

We stopped at John's restaurant, his reason for moving to Mongolia. John's business seemed like the only breath of effort put into this city. We ate his "special" pesto pasta and ordered in "Mr. Chicken," or KFC, as we call it in America.

"Okay, guys, a shot to Daria." John proclaimed in a triumphant voice.

"I'm pretty jet-lagged, guys. I think I would rather just go to the room and chill," I responded.

"What the fuck? No way! We are going to the clubs after this. Now drink your shot, you pussy."

His cousins and business partner Steve, a short, dark-skinned boy from Canada, brought out Chinggis vodka, named after the warrior and emperor, and started pouring shots into paper cups. I couldn't back down after the teasing.

There I was—sitting at the only table in a half-finished restaurant with sawdust-covered floors and with the exception of John, a bunch of strangers. It blew my mind to think that only hours ago, I was surrounded by my closest family members.

After a few shots, the tension wore off and I felt less tired. Even though it was a Tuesday night, we headed straight for the club. Its dazzling colored lights and modern furniture staged in a large warehouse trumped my expectations. This confounded my preconception of what Mongolia had to offer. Immediately, I brought the first decent-looking girls I saw to our "table," which required no bottle service (and if it did, the bottle would have been no more than eighteen dollars). They spoke no English but we danced with them and bought them drinks. They were taken aback by my straightforwardness. Obviously, they were not expecting such an experience for a Tuesday night.

"What is your phone number?" I yelled above the music. John translated.

The girl I was talking to seemed to tolerate my aggressive behavior. That is, letting me grind her on the dance floor (which I thought would be frowned upon in a conservative country such as Mongolia).

I brought her back to the table and communicated the only way I could: touch. I rubbed her neck and told John to translate in his broken Mongolian: "You're beautiful." She was eating it up. I invited her back to his restaurant and though she wanted to come, her friend was reluctant because no other guy in my group could market himself as an enticing choice.

We were forced to cut our losses and leave. I returned home with the next best thing—Steve.

Steve was gracious enough to let me use the extra bed in his hotel room.

We arrived to a tiny, cramped room, where the shower was more like a coffin with asbestos dripping from the ceiling like a leaky water faucet. I wondered how anyone could live in such a place permanently, or as long as Steve had (roughly eight months) without contracting some disease or illness.

Steve was an interesting fellow. He studied math and while he spoke with conviction, I could sense that he was plagued with uncertainty deep down. He sounded as lost as I was in this Mongolian city. He always thought he was onto an idea, believing it was the next biggest way to become a billionaire.

Steve moved to Mongolia from Canada to take an eight-month job opportunity in finance. He spent most of the day at work writing programs and, in exchange, they paid him minimally and gave him the hotel room where we stayed.

I only managed four hours of sleep that night. In the morning I rolled over, catching sight of a bag stuffed to the brim. I was stubbornly reluctant to ever open it.

*Well, you're backpacking now, you better suck it up.*

I put on the same clothes I had worn since I left home.

＝ 4 ＝

Steve and I made a beeline for Michelle's French bakery, when he told me about Kevin, his friend who was organizing a countryside safari to observe a tribe of reindeer herders many believe to be related to Native Americans. As we ate our breakfast crepes, Kevin coincidentally showed up with his little dog Panda and didn't miss a beat sharing details about his forthcoming trip. This smooth-talking Belgian, who could have passed for a titled Englishman, was twenty-seven and had been doing double duty in real estate and as a fire regulations inspector in Mongolia.

Afterward, he invited us to his well-appointed Soviet-style apartment with its four different front door locks (a chain, two bolts, and a door lock), which was just a block away and large enough to easily accommodate a ping pong table, spacious kitchen, and three bedrooms. His girlfriend, Amka, was the only other occupant so I didn't hesitate to accept his offer to spend the night away from a cramped motel room with Steve. The other little bonus was that should I choose to join him on the excursion, I would be sharing a tent with a young American woman from New York City. However, I didn't know at the time that with Kevin, nothing is at it seems.

Kevin was the ideal host for the first few days, taking me to the local supermarket and buying any and everything I wanted, including ingredients for spaghetti with meat sauce as well as dessert and wine. We spent the afternoon cooking together, drank wine, and we went sightseeing around a couple of nearby Mongolian museums. This was more than John had done in over a month.

Upon her arrival, I met the American woman—Tara—who was the opposite of what I expected. She was a red-haired teacher who would not stop prattling on about the most irrelevant, pointless stories. With her sitting next to me, I anticipated it would be a tight squeeze in the car, and after a few hours on the road that starts to really become an issue. However, despite her endless stream of stories, she did seem nice—or so I thought.

The last couple who would join us, Ben and Helen, came late the night before our departure. In the morning, only Amka and Tara were in the kitchen.

"Where's everyone? I thought we were supposed to leave in an hour," I asked Tara.

"Ben has an issue with his appendix and needed to go to the hospital," Tara replied nonchalantly.

A Mongolian doctor earns no more than two hundred dollars a month. If he chose to join us, Ben would be playing with his life as his ante in the risky game of healthcare here.

Happily, Ben came back ready to go. Giving no indication that anything was wrong with him, he was as giddy as a first grader on a field trip to the zoo. We headed outside Kevin's apartment with all our bags to find a black and a forest green Toyota Land Cruiser stocked with gear, food, and essentials waiting for us. Two hours behind schedule, we headed out of Ulaanbaatar. Our group consisted of Tara, Ben and Helen, Kevin, Amka, Panda, the driver and his wife (Baska and Bymbaa), and me.

We had a three-day drive to the camp, which would take us to the Tsatans—more popularly known as the "Reindeer People." From the stories I heard about him, Hamid, the owner of the camp, was Persian, had lived in Nepal for thirteen years, had earned his doctorate from Harvard, and was now filming documentaries for the National Geographic and Discovery cable networks. He seemed like the most relevant person I could envision meeting on the whole trip and I considered it fate that he was accessible on my path.

The drive was not boring as concrete roads became progressively more primitive until they were grassy fields matted down by tire tracks. Landscape venues changed drastically from green to dry, cold to hot, and rivers to dry creek beds. I enjoyed doing nothing with thoughts running freely and music blasting on my headphones. By nightfall, we found a *ger* camp to spend the night.

The second day was more of the same, but this time, there were not even dirt roads. It was simply fields of grass and steppes. Directions were quaintly folksy: "Head in that direction for about twenty kilometers, then go over the hill and drive through the river; pass the horses on your right." Our car broke down in the middle of a plain and while I feared that there was no help for miles, Baska, who could disassemble and reassemble the engine of any car, quickly crawled under the car and was able to fix it in no time.

The second night, we stopped at a *ger* camp that claimed to serve French and Italian food. *Lonely Planet* said it was a must-see destination. We were disappointed that the actual place was anything but must-see, especially in the dark. The chefs had left for the rest of the year so we unloaded our own pasta and cooked it ourselves.

We sipped heavily on wine to ease the pain of how cold, tired, and hungry we really were.

On the third day, the boredom began to creep in so we pulled out the guns. We stopped in an open field to shoot at a target we fashioned out of cardboard. While I was the novice Bay Area boy when it came to guns, both Kevin and Ben, who attended military schools, were quite familiar with shooting. Baska, being a Mongolian raised in the countryside, had as much familiarity as Kevin and Ben.

We drove into nightfall and although some members of our group were not keen on continuing our drive into the night, the majority won out and we continued on until we finally made it to Hamid's camp, only to find that he wasn't even there.

"Where is Hamid?" I asked desperately.

I couldn't get a straight answer out of anyone. From what I gathered after fifteen minutes of interviews, Hamid had ventured out with another group to see the Tsatans. Instead, Batsitsik greeted us in a candlelit *ger* serving as the kitchen. Batsitsik was a chef who looked like a well-kept city girl with her trendy jeans and pullovers, capped by a short but trendy haircut. She obviously paid attention to the little things in her appearance that most Mongolians from the countryside wouldn't consider. We ate and were ready to pass out as it was late and we had been on the road for three days. Our *gers* had no floors—just exposed grass and dirt. However, the beds and comforters were luxurious enough to meet our spoiled Western standards.

After three days, patience was not on my side and I was anxious to join up with Hamid's group. I called a camp guide who was willing to arrange a horse for me to ride, though he didn't look like he would abide a modern city boy who had no real experience in the wild.

"How far is Hamid?" I tried my best to communicate using some form of what I thought was universal sign language.

He understood what I meant to say and managed to explain that he was either six hours or two days away by horse. For a guy who had never ridden a horse before, that is like the difference between a blue-collar prison and Guantanamo Bay: either way I was fucked, but at least one would be less painful.

I decided to sack up and go for it despite Bymbaa's warnings. She told me that my legs would hurt and we would be camping outside in the cold and rain (we were only about sixty miles from Siberia and it was clearly no longer the summer season).

My courage faltered. I decided to stall.

"Let me ride around a little to get a feel for it."

After what seemed like an hour, I came back with a sore ass. Six hours would be quite tough.

"How long was that, Bymbaa?"

"Ten minutes."

I would not make it but I didn't want to confirm the guide's beliefs that I was not man enough for the challenge. So, I bought myself more time, telling him that we would leave early the next day, as it was already 1:00 PM.

After a couple hours, I heard one of the camp employees screaming, "Hamid! Hamid!" I looked over the vast valley and saw a tall man riding his brown horse across the river. The view of the camp was phenomenal and this scene with Hamid's arrival was straight out of a movie.

The camp overlooked a pristine green valley, completely devoid of human impact—other than our camp—with a river flowing right down the middle. The sun had begun to set in the backdrop of the valley as Hamid crossed over to our side of the bank. From the distance, he exuded confidence and elegance, somewhat like a modern-day version of a Renaissance European explorer—complete with a rounded brown chapeau, knee-high brown leather boots (the kind Hermes makes and all the young women wear though they don't actually ride horses), and a dark green blazer.

When Kevin introduced us, I was awestruck, speechless to meet the embodiment of all that I wanted to be. I was almost as giddy as when I met Leonardo (the blue Ninja Turtle) at my third birthday party. Only now I was seeing a real-time life-sized version of the hero I always had imagined. He was a Persian Harvard graduate who had spent years learning from Nepalese monks about Buddhism and I thought he would understand the essence of what I was yearning for.

I had so many questions and ideas to share, wishing that he could just know it all right away. Despite my excitement, I didn't want to seem desperate, so I kept quiet. Hamid was a little chubbier than I expected and growing bald. But I didn't want to let physical appearances deceive me.

"Yes, the *feng shui* of this location is fantastic. You have the river flowing toward you in the valley and the sun setting behind it. The energy received is tremendous," he said with the poise and authority of a wise old teacher.

With every word, I was more impressed.

"You see those flags? They were blessed by the Dalai Lama."

"What are those horses?" I asked him.

"Those are wind horses."

He had even met the Dalai Lama. I wished this guy would be my lifetime mentor.

After his arrival, four others came on horseback— a young man named Raoul, his girlfriend Victoria, and two older women: Judith and Despina. Victoria was a gorgeous, well-educated American and when she talked, you could tell she was well traveled. She spoke with fiery conviction. Yet, she seemed down to earth and philosophical. In many ways, she embodied the perfect woman. Raoul was a tall, skinny, and bearded South African national. He was not the Spanish-speaking charming character of Juan Antonio in *Vicky Christina Barcelona* played by Javier Bardem that I expected. He was, however, very easygoing and was not too strongly opinionated about anything.

The other two women acted very French (they lived in Paris even though they were from Greece and America): seductive and pretentious. They were snooty, exuding an aura of haughtiness that did keep them distant from the others in the camp. One who looked to be in her sixties, Judith, could have passed for an older version of Barbra Streisand with her long blonde curly locks. The other, Despina, was curvaceous, in her forties, and nearly perfect except for some gaps between her teeth.

That first night, I managed a great buzz, thanks to the wine and a fantastic conversation with Despina about life. The conversation carried on through dinner as Hamid overheard everything, seeming impressed at my insight.

*Finally, my hero was getting to know me,* indirectly, of course. *Maybe he could unveil some divine truths for me . . .*

"You remind me of me when I was young," Hamid said.

At that point, I was shocked at how egotistical one could be with a compliment, which seems like an oxymoron, yet somehow he got away with it. It was a discreet, unnoticed form of vanity. And yet, I was still willing to overlook it. I was placed on the same playing field as my hero—by my hero. To me, it was one of the greatest possible compliments I would ever hear.

Once everyone left for bed other than Raoul, Hamid, and me, I couldn't control myself any longer.

"So how was your experience in Nepal?" I blurted out. I remembered that he had spent thirteen years studying in Nepal.

"That conversation will have to be saved for another night," he said with a chuckle. That night never came.

## 5

The next morning a local shaman was at our camp performing rituals, and she pulled out small pebbles of
earth-tone colors from a colorful pouch to use for making
predictions. Though Bymbaa's translation, she predicted
that I would marry within the next year and have a child.
Then, I would return to this camp. She also knew of my
late friend, Will, who I continued to think much about.
It had not yet been a year since his death but her mention
of him touched me deeply. She suggested that she contact
his spirit for me at midnight. I was taken aback by the
strange offer but still curious about its implications. I left
the *ger* in a trance.

My ride to find Hamid and the Tsatans was replaced
with the less-than-noble ride to find the local vodka
maker. Before leaving, though, two Tsatans showed up
with several reindeers, which, because of their size, were
not meant to be ridden by anyone weighing more than
150 pounds. Standing four feet tall with velvet horns, soft
brown fur, and white neck markings, they appeared to
be much less sturdy than horses. We crossed the river in
a small inflatable, packing in as many people as dangerously possible, to catch a closer look at these magnificent
creatures with their velvet horns.

"Can I ride one?" I asked Baska.

"Yes, wait." Before I was able to ride, Tara, Kevin, and Ben had a shot.

I jumped on the reindeer once they finished their merry-go-round of a ride with a Tsatan pulling it by a rope, like a pony at a kid's birthday party. But after several steps, the creature buckled under me, so I jumped off to avoid injuring both myself and the reindeer. The Tsatan didn't seem too preoccupied.

The Tsatans showed us their campsite, which was barely more than a large rag that had been scattered on the ground. On the rag stood a pot of fermented reindeer milk and some cheese—the typical diet out in the wilderness. They slept with no shelter or blanket in the near-freezing temperatures, battling the cold with their own thick skin.

My curiosity got the best of me and I tried a taste of the reindeer milk, which was far better than its thick, yellowish appearance suggested. More than anything, it tasted like water. Then I went for the cheese, whose sharp, astringent taste got stuck in my throat. It took me several minutes to get the aftertaste out of my mouth.

Having nourished my giddy need to see the reindeer, I hopped on a horse just in time to follow Hamid to the vodka maker along with Baska, Bymbaa, and Victoria. Feeling adventurous, I suggested we traipse through the forest and with that Hamid zipped off with Victoria. That was the first glimpse I got of Hamid's character as a host.

My horse would not completely abide my commands and there was little I could do about it. Luckily, Baska and Bymbaa—who seemed more like loving parents or, even better, heaven-sent angels—followed close behind me, watching every move.

We struggled through the forest that left us only narrow paths and thick canopies of tree branches to dodge and duck under, trying to remain near the river in order to avoid getting completely lost within the damp forests. We emerged into the clearing on a gravel road littered with trash, and in the distance we could see a set of white *gers* nestled in the valley. We strode toward the hut, thinking that it would be the only logical place for Hamid to be. Finally, we caught up to Hamid and Victoria, who were close to a *ger*.

"There is a local shaman here who is highly respected. You should pay him a visit," Hamid suggested.

So, without hesitation, we galloped to his *ger* instead of seeing the vodka maker. We entered a small *ger* adorned with dozens of brightly colored red, blue, and green shaman scarves hanging from the ceiling. I watched the shaman placing powder into flat paper.

"What kind of ritual is this?" I asked Hamid.

"Rolling a cigarette," Hamid said with more than a hint of mocking laughter.

I felt utterly stupid. Shamans were normal people after all. The short man sat in eerie silence and smoked, his dark face and clothes covered with a thick layer of dust, as we watched. No rush, no care. Afterwards, he draped something with several shamanic scarves and held a carved wooded idol and gently placed them on the floor between us. He blew into a miniature metal instrument I had never seen before. It had one string and when picked it emanated an eerily robotic sound. He focused intently for a while, interpreting the sound, before speaking again.

"Your friend is always surrounding you and wants to take you to the other side with him. You must come back tonight. Will you?" Hamid translated his remarks for me.

"Sure," I said with a bit of skepticism.

"This shaman is more competent than the woman you met earlier," Hamid assured me.

"Okay, I'll come tonight."

"You must bring chocolates, a pack of cigarettes, thirty dollars, and a bottle of vodka for the ceremony."

It was as if I was slapped out of a trance. Cigarettes? Vodka? What a fool I was to go along with this.

"Hamid, I don't want to do this," I said, with protest loud in my tone.

"You can't say no. You must go, it's too late."

Obviously impatient, Hamid didn't want to upset the shaman. I had no choice.

Back at the camp, I told everyone about the shaman ritual and they were eager to witness it. Rather than provide the shaman with a bottle of vodka and a pack of cigarettes, I opted to fill a small water bottle with vodka and cached three cigarettes courtesy of Despina.

While we sat around waiting for dinner, a Tsatan showed up frighteningly drunk. His eyes were bloodshot as he barged into the "living room" of the ger. Hamid had scurried under the table, trying to avoid any contact.

"Hamid!" the Tsatan yelled incoherently, unable to spot Hamid.

Raoul escorted the belligerent drunk, who stumbled out the door. The inebriated intruder tried to push against the door and the ger shook with every motion. It seemed that the structure would collapse. We were in a daze, shocked at Hamid's incapacity to take charge. The Tsatan continued to pound on the door, yelling ferociously. Then there was abrupt silence.

About fifteen minutes later, the drunken tribesman returned while we sat at the table, eating dessert.

"Hamid!" He yelled again.

"Don't let him through," Hamid told me as I sat between him and the Tsatan behind the table. He stood over me, yelling at me to move, but I refused. As he shouted louder, the Tsatan's spit covered more of my food and my face, so I ignored Hamid's plea for me to act as a human blockade and let the drunk Tsatan through. Completely disappointed in Hamid, I couldn't believe how he had abdicated his duty as camp host. The group left Hamid and the Tsatan alone while the rest of us headed for the cars in preparation for the shaman ritual.

It was pouring rain as we drove through the footpaths of the darkened forest. At the *ger*, everything was so dark I couldn't see my own hand in front of my face. Apparently, the room had to be completely dark for the ritual. Once all ten of us were settled in, the shaman commanded me to come forth. The spotlight was trained on me and candles illuminated the exchange with the shaman, who pulled out his now-familiar one-stringed metal instrument. Preparing for a trance, he tuned himself to the vibrations of the spirit world, drank some vodka, and reached for his mask. His wife and son helped him don his costume, which resembled what native Americans might wear—a sheepskin jacket and boots with strands dangling from the arms like confetti, but longer. His mask was scary even in its brightly colored features; there was what looked like colorful hair around the mask. Holding a drum the size of a basketball in his hand with a baton, he was like a warrior ready for battle. His motions were unpredictable as he stood in front of me and began to chant, singing and dancing wildly. Everyone in the *ger* watched with the widest eyes, so as not to miss a moment. He banged the drum on my head, not very concerned with how much it might hurt.

During the ritual, which lasted no more than ten minutes, vivid memories of my dead friend gushed forward. I could see his face smiling at me, the times we spent in the gym together or played video games. I couldn't stop the tears from rolling down my cheeks, crying over my fallen friend in this shaman's *ger* in the middle of nowhere in Mongolia while nine strangers watched intently.

The shaman eventually wrapped up the ceremony and his wife helped him pull his costume off. He yelled and as soon as his wife took off his mask he collapsed on the ground. The wife didn't look the least bit worried, so I assumed everything had gone as planned. As he swooned, his wife and son grabbed him and placed him on the ground where he slowly regained his composure. The shaman eventually rejoined the group, now fully in control of himself, explaining to all those who could understand the Mongolian dialect about the conclusion of his journey to the other world. He spoke for a few minutes and I waited patiently for the translation.

"You were going to die but he saved you," Kevin told me. I waited for more.

"That's it?"

"Yes, and your friend was going to kill you."

"What?"

"Your friend spirit want to take you to other world with him. Now shaman save you," Baska explained, definitely more concerned with what had transpired than Kevin.

On the drive back, I gathered from Baska that my friend was going to arrange for my death in the spring so that I could join him in the other world. However, because of this ceremony, his spirit would no longer hang over me, meaning my death has been postponed until further notice.

Deeply moved, I remained silent on the drive back. However, the more I pondered what the shaman said and how he had claimed that my friend was trying to kill me, the more upset I became at how immature this string of events sounded. Why would a divine soul be so greedy? Especially since I had viewed him as my protector. I concluded that the shaman was full of shit.

## 6

The following morning, I marched to the tent that housed the small, plastic, portable toilet. Inside waited a large dog—maybe eighty pounds with the thickness and size of a Siberian husky and the colors of a German shepherd. The dog had a pair of tan spots above its eyes believed to allow the dog to see and ward off evil spirits. I sat on the toilet and suddenly the dog rose on all fours and came to me.

*Oh shit, I offended him. I moved into his territory. You're gonna get it and your pants are down.*

He gently placed his head between my legs and left it there. "No!" I yelled and pushed his head away, only to find that he returned his nose between my legs and continued to stare at me. It seemed as if he just wanted to rest in my lap. Though I normally wouldn't mind, I found it quite odd that this was happening while I was sitting on a small portable plastic toilet with my pants down. I gave up on pushing the dog away and tried to ignore him.

When things couldn't get any worse, I looked up and focused my eyes on an empty roll of toilet paper. My heart dropped. It was like a scene out of *Dumb and Dumber* and though it wasn't the most pleasurable of experiences, it was the most memorable of all my toilet memories.

Outside the tent, Hamid and the camp guide were saddling up their horses for a ride around the valley. I hopped on one of the saddled horses and after a short trot with them, I decided to split and explore on my own. I put on my headphones and found myself in a different landscape. The drizzle of rain splashed gently upon my face as I watched the sun settle lower against the backdrop of this lush valley, as perfect as one could imagine heaven on earth. The cool, crisp air brushed more intensely against my chilled cheeks the faster I galloped aimlessly around the valley, taking in the extraordinary landscape with all my senses.

My reverie halted abruptly when my horse stopped and turned around in fear. I leaned over the horse to get a glimpse of what had stopped him. A fallen animal lay strewn across the grassy field, a justifiably startling sight for the horse and me. The carcass was a half-eaten horse whose insides were splayed across a broad section of ground cover. The frozen façade of the carcass spoke terror and I remembered hearing earlier that day about a pack of wolves that attacked a camp. I could not escape the haunting image the remainder of the day.

≈

After a couple days at camp, I finally decided it was time for a bath. Outside the designated bath *ger*, two four-foot-high metal trash bins were filled with water from the river and placed over a fire. Tubes traveled from these bins carrying water to a pair of tubs inside the *ger* that were more suitable for intimate purposes than for a lonely, grubby backpacker. Inside the tent was a massage room as one might see on the Travel Channel. I half expected a gorgeous masseuse to come in and cater to my every aching bone. Except no one came. I stepped in the tub, less than a quarter full.

"Ahhhh!" I screamed.

The water was almost boiling. It didn't occur to me that that might have been the reason they had placed a bucket of cold water next to the tubs.

Though the water was a vague brownish hue with numerous bits and strands of hairs floating in it from all the previous users, I surmounted my hesitation because of my desperate need to get clean in whatever manner possible. Without the benefit of a shower head continuously shooting streams of fresh water over my body, I was forced to recycle the water to clean my hair and body while I stood in the tub. I was cleaning myself with my own dirt but being too picky would have meant forfeiting the opportunity to enjoy this strangely luxurious setting in the middle of nowhere.

≈

With the camp experience ending, the departures became quite emotional. The whole gang had lined up to bid us farewell as we loaded up the last of our mostly consumed belongings. The woman shaman began crying, followed by the vodka maker, and the horse guide who had initially characterized me as a pansy. As they urged me to return next summer, I realized how much this camp had become like family to me in just four days.

The horse guide, who I thought judged me as weak and incompetent, approached me. "You heart . . . " and he burst into tears as he hugged me. He didn't need to say anything more.

≈

We inherited Batsitsik for the drive back to Ulaanbaatar, as she had to get back there as well. Hamid left before any of us woke that morning.

After a few hours, we stood and waited for the second car. Twenty minutes passed and still no sign of it. We grew worried and retraced our route to find Kevin, Tara, Ben, Amka, and Panda standing outside of their vehicle with a dent running down the entire side and a flat tire.

"What happened?" I asked Kevin.

"The car flipped," he mentioned this as if it were no big deal.

"How did you manage to get it back up?"

"Well, twenty Mongolians came out of nowhere and helped straighten the car out with ropes and sheer man-power. Then they disappeared just as quickly," he said, in the most casual tone possible.

Tara appeared to be the most shocked of the group, looking pale and ready to faint. Apparently, she didn't have her seatbelt on when the accident happened and everything tumbled on her when the car toppled on its side, including pots of butter and Panda.

"They told me to hand over Panda and the butter before they helped me out!" she whined. Baska, our driver and mechanic, was seeing if the car was safe to drive and after a five-minute inspection, he gave his okay. He was quite nonchalant, despite the fact that his car had been severely damaged. Given the aggressive way Kevin drove, it was not surprising that eventually something would happen to this overstressed vehicle. Baska changed the tire in less than five minutes and we piled back in our respective cars as if nothing had happened. But, after a short while, we glanced back to see the second car growing more distant. We backtracked again to find the car was disabled because of yet another flat tire.

Baska needed to get creative. We had no more spares, so he placed the bad tire under the car's axle after jacking it up and then lowered the jack, using the car's weight to deflate the tire. He then separated the tire from the rim, placed stones in the gap to prevent the tire from popping back into place, and removed the tire off the rim. From inside the tire, he pulled out the tube and replaced it with a new one. We each took turns with the hand pump, and it took about 1,500 pumps to inflate the tire sufficiently. The process, however, only took about thirty minutes, because Baska was so efficient.

This event repeated itself several more times. Three flat tires later, day had faded into night and we had no more tubes left. This time, Baska had to do all of the above plus patch the tube, which required him to search for the hole by pouring water all along the half-inflated tube. Once he found the hole, he patched it and sanded it down before placing it back in the tire. After the patchwork we were off, only to stop again five hundred feet further down.

Baska got out again and did all the work with saintly patience and though we tried to help, he would not let us. No trace of anger or frustration existed in this phenomenally calm man. But our plan wasn't working.

"Why doesn't one car just go to the town and get help?" I asked Kevin.

"I don't want to split up the cars in case of an emergency."

"Isn't this an emergency?"

An hour later, Kevin, Amka, and I volunteered to stay with the car while the rest headed for town to get help.

"Can we put up the tent?" I asked Baska.

"No! Many wolf!" Baska warned in an uncharacteristically urgent tone.

Instead, they handed me the rifle, a bottle of gin, and my sleeping bag while the others went to town—which, at best, was a two-hour drive despite it being just fifty miles away. I slept in the back of the car while Kevin and Amka passed out in front. We didn't drink or move; we were stuck in the middle of the valley with no one for miles and no other option but to sleep until they came back.

I woke in the middle of the night with the urge to relieve myself. I climbed out of the car, pointing my flashlight in every direction, fearing a wolf was staring me straight in the face or standing behind me. Two headlights were coming towards me in the distance. *It must be some locals driving through*, I thought as I went on with my business. The lights got closer until they came up right behind me. *Now this is embarrassing.* I turned to find Baska and Bymbaa—my real heroes were there to rescue me.

Bymbaa took me to town while Baska changed the tire on the lemon car. It was past 2:00 AM. We had spent over five hours in that miserable car in the cold. I slept the whole way to town, despite my neck yanking back and forth from the bumpy road.

We headed out again after lunch the following day with breathtaking views of the Mongolian countryside lighting up our windows like a movie screen—long expansive green plains stretching over hilltops that would reveal equally verdant valleys nearly as perfect as those in a carefully composed landscape painting. We saw volcanoes and piles upon piles of black volcano rocks, lakes, forests, plains, and, of course, steppes. At times, I had a hard time remembering what country I was visiting.

## 7

We averaged about three to four flat tires a day—usually one in the morning and two others throughout the day, each one setting us back over an hour. It was
frustrating but expected. Mongolian roads were among
the worst to be encountered. Road signs were virtually
nonexistent. Following the only sign that indicated we
had traveled hundreds of miles on the accurate route,
we arrived at a delightful *ger* camp by a lake. There were
other pleasant moments. At one stop, Baska somehow
managed to recognize his father's friend's *ger* despite not
having been there in twenty years. He went in for a visit
and, in exchange, the residents loaded us up with cream
of milk and *airag* (fermented mare's milk). It was a suitable substitute for a formal meal.

We continued on, crossing a three-foot-deep river.
We eventually followed a set of footpaths down the side
of a mountain through the mud until we drove out into a
clearing and came upon another *ger* camp. As we set up
camp, everyone moved their backpacks and belongings
into the *gers* as Baska worked on his car using a powerful
search lamp for light.

"You want wolf hunt?" he asked me spontaneously.

"Of course!" I answered.

He pointed his search lamp toward the hills about 300
feet away when a set of piercing blue eyes looked back.

"Blue eyes. It's wolf . . . " Baska confirmed.

I couldn't believe it. We were sleeping in this *ger* camp and, just a few feet away, wolves were watching us. With Ben, we loaded up the rifles and headed into the hills with guns aimed out of the windows. They knew we were coming and were well hidden. We searched for about fifteen minutes when we spotted one lounging in the distance. Baska turned off his car as Ben and I held our guns out the window in complete silence, breaths held.

Before I could coordinate, Ben shot at the animal and began sprinting toward it maniacally. He disappeared in the darkness. I watched the wolf run off unscathed. Our predicament was quite unusual, with Ben running after a wolf on foot, and Baska and I driving to find him. We found him huffing and puffing but also as ecstatic as a fourth grader going to Disneyland for the first time. "This is awesome!"

We woke up the next morning and continued driving to Ulaanbaatar, finally hitting a concrete road several hours into the drive. At that point, we were able to gun it and head straight for the capital. Baska no longer had to slow every thirty feet for bumps and in two hours we covered the distance that we had previously accomplished in eight hours.

Despite the numerous hiccups in traveling, I gained an appreciation for the unexpected pleasures of frequent stops and patience in delaying the schedule. I was surprised at how I had overpowered my habitual compulsion to seek out control and comfort. I was willing to set that aside in order to realize my dreams.

$$\approx 8 \approx$$

When I returned, John was waiting with a bottle of black Chinggis vodka. "It's your last day; we're getting hammered."

He didn't need to say more before we had finished the first bottle of vodka for the night. My idea was to stop at every cool bar along the way to Hazara, an Indian restaurant. With Amelie, Cyrile, a French couple we had met at John's restaurant, and John tagging along, I headed out to the first stop—the new piano bar in town.

Judging from the emptiness of the bar, we were the only ones looking for a drink at three in the afternoon. John ordered us all Red Bull vodkas to get us started. I finished my drink and most of Amelie's, too. And before long, we were off to the next bar. On the street, John mentioned how wasted we were while it was still daytime. As if we weren't drunk enough, we stopped at another bar next door. I remembered thinking that I would never make it across town at this rate. The bar was dark and claustrophobic—like a pub in an old mystery movie.

"Four Red Bull vodkas," I screamed at the bartender.

I vaguely remember telling the bartender to blast Michael Jackson while I stood in the middle of the bar and tried to moonwalk. Then the image of me giving a speech came back. John was moved to tears as I told him I loved him like a brother. The French guests looked on with compassion. And then, blackout.

I returned to consciousness in a karaoke room singing Ricky Martin at the top of my lungs. I picked up a drink I knew wasn't mine. My mind was screaming to me that I had already finished mine. Back to black.

Then I stood in the entrance of John's restaurant as his entire family—mother, cousins, and aunts included—looked shocked at our state of inebriation. Back to black.

I was in John's restaurant bathroom trying to hold John up so he could puke. Back to black.

I sat in a car with people trying to calm me even as I told them I was okay. Back to black. Even my soul didn't want to stick around for this, and it left my drunken body.

I woke up in a bed next to Amelie.

*Oh shit! Please no! I hope I didn't . . .*

I turned over, coming face to face with John's wide open mouth.

*Phew!*

Behind Amelie, I saw Cyrile. All of us had passed out in Amelie and Cyrile's hotel room bed. Still drunk, I assumed that I had not puked last night. I had to awaken everybody and get us going to the airport. The last thing I wanted was to miss my flight out of Mongolia. After two months here, I had had enough.

When the phone rang, John grudgingly answered it. It was his mom.

"My mom was at the restaurant last night?" he asked me in a groggy voice.

"I don't know," I said.

"She's asking me why I was so drunk." He laughed. "Mom, I got to go." He hung up.

Amelie, who had been the most sober among the group, recounted the events of the previous night.

"Daria, you were pulling on the karaoke staff's hair to get them to bring you drinks! John couldn't keep up with you and you tried to run off into the street! Cyrile was puking outside John's restaurant, telling me how much he loves me and that he'd never been that drunk before. After karaoke, we went to another bar. You ordered fifteen vodkas and countless beers. You spilled some of them and sent some back and then continued drinking. Then you snatched the bill from the waitress and tore it up! They had to bring a new one."

She paused for a moment to gauge our reactions.

"Obviously, we never made it to Hazara. I made sure you had everything and offered to have you guys at our hotel. All of John's family was there and saw you guys. John's cousin will be here to pick us up. Then I took off all your shoes and tucked you in . . . "

"I have to vomit," John interrupted as he ran to the toilet.

John's cousin never showed up so we jumped into a taxi. Amelie continued telling us stories of the previous night as we laughed hysterically at each other's clumsy behavior.

At the airport, John tried to be discreet as he looked around and then stuck his finger in his throat on the edge of the street. He aimed over the edge of the departure bridge and unloaded below on the arrivals section. His hair was mussed up terribly, as if he had just battled a storm. Frankly, all of us were a mess. I kept my eye on the nearest trash can at all times in case pangs of nausea hit me.

As we said our goodbyes, Amelie cried and reached into her purse to give me the only thing she had—Chanel No. 5 perfume.

"What do I do with this?" I asked her.

"You put this on last night. And . . . I want you to have it."

John admitted that he wanted to cry as well but was too afraid that he would vomit if he did. Cyrile was simply lost. I said goodbye one final time and turned to leave.

I didn't have time in my drunken haze to print out my electronic itinerary, which would prove to be a problem several times throughout the coming day. The immigration officials couldn't fathom an idiot who would simply not print out an itinerary.

At the Mongolian immigration control point, the woman behind the counter looked at my passport four times as if it indicated that I was a known criminal. She sent me to a guy who took me to another man in a suit. It definitely was getting official. My breath still reeked of alcohol and I looked like death. The chubby man appeared to be friendly enough and I still had the added ounce of alcoholic courage.

"Come with me," he said without another word.

I followed him into his floor-to-ceiling glass-surrounded office, where he had photo posters of terrorists hanging on the windows. All the passengers by the gate could see inside.

"Well, you stayed over thirty days . . . "

"Yeah, I'm allowed ninety," I responded, quickly hoping to ward off his attack.

"But you need to fill out an extension form."

"It doesn't say anything about that anywhere."

"It's Mongolian law. Now the fee is 250,000 *tugriks* [$170]."

Still hammered, I decided to bargain.

"Well, I have no money."

"Then you will have to leave tomorrow."

"Do you accept VISA?"

"Cash only."

"Well, I'll make you a deal. I can give you 100,000 *tugriks* to let me go right now. That's the most I can give you."

"This is not a business. You are dealing with the government of Mongolia!"

"Alright, I'll give you 150,000 *tugriks*."

"Okay."

"Okay. Is there an ATM?"

We headed through various security checkpoints to the ATM and then passed through security on our return. The Mongolian equivalent of the TSA patted me down, instructing me to empty my jacket pocket. I was surprised when I pulled out a passion fruit blunt wrap I had completely forgotten about, which I handed to the guy.

"It's good shit," I told the security guy, who looked at it as if it were an alien object. The security officers looked at me, puzzled, and before they could say anything, I disappeared.

Back at the office, my "new friend" collected my 150,000 *tugriks*. I knew he wasn't a mean guy. As I paid my citation, I joked with the man about how hammered I still was from the night before. He led me to my gate and within a short time, I was out of Mongolia and relieved at the fact.

At the Beijing airport, I waited in the transfer line with the worst hangover. I felt like I was going to fall down in place. The anxiety of being completely alone for the first time and hungover made me almost vomit several times.

Once I got to the front, they asked for my electronic ticket.

"I don't have one."

"No E-ticket?!"

"No."

He sent me to another line where the woman asked the same question and I gave the same response. She looked up from her paperwork for the first time during our conversation as if she had never had to deal with such an incompetent traveler in her career. She picked up the phone and tried to confirm my itinerary and then stamped my passport, obviously happy to get me out of the way.

The entire ride on the plane, which lasted more than five hours (and thanks to my newfound patience, it felt more like a drive to the nearest Safeway), I stared at the barf bag, which silently taunted me to do the deed. Because Panda (Kevin's dog) had eaten my headphones, I had to use a set the airline provided for my iPod. Listening out of one ear and barely hearing anything, I still felt lucky to be enjoying music in any form.

My next stop was in Malaysia, where for the first time in two months, I saw my taste in women and brand-name stores. In fact, for the first time, I saw brands I actually recognized. I enjoyed my brief respite in this commercial paradise. I purchased a set of high-end headphones and authentic Energizer batteries that lasted longer than three minutes and cost more than ten cents. I was ready for sleep, as it already had been a long day and, even worse, I was still enduring the worst possible hangover. Unfortunately, every room at the interior airport hotel was booked.

I had no choice but to leave the airport and find another hotel during my eight-hour layover. I found one close enough and checked in as I let my body go into deep relaxation. A welcome treat was the opportunity to watch television for the first time in two months. It didn't matter what was on the set. I just appreciated the momentary pleasure of living vicariously through some banal icon of American pop culture.

The rest had cured my hangover and had energized me for the ongoing anxiety of the unpredictable nature of international travel. New batteries in my iPod and a shower refreshed me (as did the ability to brush my teeth for the first time in three days). A complete reset was definitely in order.

The best virtue I carried from Mongolia was patience. The endless parade of flat tires and car troubles as well as seemingly interminable waits for doing everything that I had hoped to do tested my patience and pushed me to new levels. I had to be disciplined in unexpected ways. I learned that spending hours or days waiting—or "wasting" time—is not so bad. Time is not wasted when we are not required to produce complete efficiency every second of our lives. Boredom and delays are only as daunting as one allows them to be.

The twenty-six hour journey to Bali no longer felt like an exhausting task but a pleasant time for reflection.

≈

# PART TWO

*Bali: Interlude in Paradise*

≈

My first day in Bali, I scouted Sanur, a textbook-perfect tranquil beach town lined with quiet roads occasionally interrupted by the noise of a zippy moped. In Sanur, I was going to learn how to kite surf. I woke up at seven the next morning to take my level one course in kite surfing, which consisted mainly of philosophy and how to pack and unpack gear—nothing nearly as exciting as the videos I had watched. I was anxious to get out onto the water, but to my disappointment we never did during the ninety-minute lesson.

Fully aware how difficult it would be to find a friendly companion to enjoy this Balinese paradise, I decided to explore the island a bit after my class—thanks to the amazingly cheap rental fee of five bucks a day for a scooter. I paid the rental fee, an entire fifteen dollars for three days, and the attendent gave me the bike without asking for any paperwork or ID. All he wanted to know was what hotel I stayed at, which I could have easily lied about. I hoped the scooter rental facility had great insurance, but somehow I doubted it. Bali is an extremely trusting environment.

So I took off onto the main street, a bit nervous about driving on the left side of the road, on a bike no less. Starting to get my bearings for navigating the streets, I continued on the highway, and before long I saw a cop come up alongside me. I assumed he wanted me to pull over for speeding.

"Let me see your license."

I didn't have my license with me and legally I couldn't even drive the scooter because I didn't have an international license.

"I don't have it with me."

There was no reason for me to get pulled over— I wasn't speeding or riding without a helmet. Another policeman came and took out his citation book to write me up.

"It will cost you $200 but you can give me $20 now."

"I've only got five dollars but if you come back to my hotel, I can give you the rest", I told him, not thinking he would bite.

He was hesitant because now the tables had turned in my favor; he had to follow me and face an uncomfortable predicament, taking bribes in front of potential witnesses. But eventually he followed me and waited outside as I went into my hotel. I asked the receptionist, "I got pulled over and the cop wants money. How much should I pay him?"

"Oh, not more than five dollars!"

"But I don't have a license . . . "

"Oh! In that case, make it ten dollars!"

"He's waiting out there. Is it bad if I just don't go back to him?"

"Yes, you should pay him. He might see you one time on the road and really give you trouble."

So I went into my room and grabbed another five dollars and headed out to the street corner.

"Sorry, this is all I got," I told him as I indiscreetly gave him the ten dollars. He looked around as if his cover would be blown and grabbed the money quickly and put it away.

"I don't have an international license; can I still drive?"

"No, it's better if you don't," he warned.

I returned to my bike and, once he left, continued back on my way to a local restaurant.

～

The next day was the second for kite surfing, and body dragging was on the agenda. The instructor's aides assisted me with my harness and took me out on a small wooden boat to the reef about a mile out. There, the lead instructor showed off his moves, jumping off the waves and grabbing his board in unnecessary places while in the air to prove his expertise. Mario was a tall Italian man with a thick accent who believed he was Fabio's better-looking brother. Apparently this guy had never looked in the mirror.

"Okay, now grab the chicken loop," he explained with his thick accent, sitting next to me on the boat.

"So I grab this loop?"

"Yes, grab the loop." I looked at the red rope hanging down from the loop and pulled on it.

"Whoa! NOOOO! Not that one!"

The kite flew off into the distance, now completely detached from the harness. I had misunderstood the instructions and pulled the emergency release instead of grabbing the actual hook.

He turned the boat around and pulled the kite out of the water and, after some arduous work and frustration, we were back in the same position five minutes later.

"Okay, now grab the chicken loop and hook this on." This time, the instructions were clear.

I was supposed to be pulled along in the water while moving the kite in a specific direction to gain speed. But, without a board underneath me, the kite yanked me up out of the water, only to smack me back with the sting of a belly flop. As the kite dragged me again and again across the water, lifting me higher into the air, I noticed black rock all around me at a depth barely below the water's surface. My legs scraped along the jagged edges, bruising and lacerating as the kite dragged me across. Bleeding and now flaying out of control, I felt clumsy and vulnerable as I wobbled around, trying desperately to get control of the kite's massive power but forced to let go of the handle. Then, BAM! The kite went straight into the water.

"PULL RIGHT! RIIIIIIIIGHT!" the Italian yelled in his thick accent. It was more annoying than helpful.

As I pulled right, the kite desperately tried to follow, but it surrendered against the effort. The instructor went to the kite and lifted it out of the water.

"Pull left. LEFT!"

I pulled my bar left; the kite zipped into the air and took me out of the water to a couple of feet above the surface.

Halfway through, I finally was getting the hang of it, doing it properly without crashing the kite. Proudly, I turned around to see the instructor's face after my progress, but he was nowhere in sight. In the middle of the water, where I could see in every direction for miles, I could not find Mario. *Awesome*, I thought to myself.

The boat showed up several minutes later with another kid. The instructor had left me in the middle of my lesson to get another student: an all-American Adonis boy about my age but with golden locks, blue eyes, and a muscular physique. Grudgingly, I accepted having to share my time with him now. I hopped back in the boat as I removed my gear.

After the class, I went to the receptionist of my hotel.

"Excuse me, what day of the week is it?" I asked her.

"It's Tuesday, sir," she responded with a broad smile.

To my satisfaction, I had lost my sense of time during my travels. The days blended into each other and it became irrelevant for me what day or time it was. Time was unimportant as I had no set plans. The feeling was liberating.

I was only able to manage one more kite surfing lesson before the breezes completely died for the season.

The wind conditions didn't improve over the following days either, so it was time to change plans: if I couldn't experience the thrill of flying above water, I might as well explore the depths underwater. It was time to learn to scuba dive.

I gave the wind one last chance to allow me to kite surf, but it wasn't budging.

## ⮞ 10 ⮜

I was worried about the amount of money I'd been spending in Bali but then I came to a critical understanding. The rule of thumb in spending money is divided into two categories: experiential and commodified spending. Any money spent toward a new experience or skill was a well-chosen investment, even if I did not ultimately pursue it, whereas any dollar spent toward a commodified purchase I thought endowed me with status was a wasted allocation of funds.

My rule of thumb when making an investment was: Will it help me grow? As long as I was learning something and expanding my horizon, it was a wise investment—in myself. It is well worth considering the way we spend our funds in our world of relentless materialism.

∽

As the wind had died down, I found a surf school to embark on my new mission of learning to surf. I found a hotel closer to my surf school, which also happened to be located in a section of town bustling with entertainment and activity.

I couldn't help but realize how quickly attachments occur and how easily I settled into a comfort zone, even in an unfamiliar place. I constantly reminded myself that the art of detachment was essential to making this multinational journey effective and transformative. Already, I was second guessing my decision to move from Sanur to Kuta when I realized that the latter location had no restaurants conveniently situated on the beach. Yet I had only eaten on the beach in Sanur once since I came to Bali. It was going to take effort and will to release myself from these subconscious ruses of perception and impression. Now aware, I packed my bag—and life—in twenty minutes and was ready to move on to the next place, mind, heart, and soul completely open.

## 11

It didn't happen with a near-fatal car accident. A much less consequential incident was all I needed. Inspiration and renewals of faith come in many different forms, but mine came with a text message. Milan Kundera might refer to it as a "series of laughable fortuities." However, in my opinion, there was no chance involved.

After finishing up lunch, I returned to find my lawn chair on the beach was no longer there. When I spoke to the guy in charge, he ignored my concerns and told me to sit down next to him on the bench. Obediently, and without knowing why, I listened. Perhaps, finally tired of the temporary bonding I cultivated with waiters at restaurants, I longed for substantive human interaction. Either way I sat down and before I knew it, he was gone and I was alone again.

I put in my iPod and drifted off into my own world when three local women came and usurped my bench, sitting closer than what would be considered comfortable. Two of them sat stiffly in their uncomfortably tight-fitting jean shorts, staring at me, while the younger one looked off into the horizon. Speaking Balinese and laughing heartily, they made me insecure and I thought that I might be the object of their amusement. All three were eating greedily, their faces shoved into their bowls in between jokes.

"What are you guys eating?" I asked with genuine curiosity.

"Meatballs," the woman next to me answered.

"You must not really like your meatballs," I told her as I pointed to her empty bowl.

They all laughed and, at that instant, over a cheesy joke about meatballs, we formed what would have otherwise been an unlikely friendship.

A couple of minutes later, the same woman, Liana, sat next to me on the lawn chairs. She pulled out her phone and started texting. Though I don't like to be nosy, my eyes couldn't help but wander repeatedly to her phone screen. It read:

*"I'm sitting in my room alone and I miss you so much."*

As soon as she caught my wandering eyes, she pulled the phone towards her and out of my sight—but it was too late.

"You see! That is why I cannot have a girlfriend. There is just too much drama and lying!" I said.

Again, they all burst out laughing. The woman next to me came up with a sorry attempt at an excuse. Regardless, we enjoyed each other's company for hours until sundown.

"Come with us to church on Sunday," the mischievous woman next to me said impulsively, barely losing a beat in her phone texting.

The invitation was completely unexpected.

"Well, uh—I have surfing and scuba lessons every day until I leave. I don't think I can come."

"Well, give me your phone number and I will text you Saturday to see if you change your mind, and if you want, you can join us on Sunday."

I obliged.

The next morning I woke up and reluctantly looked at the time, hoping it was not anywhere near 7:30 AM. It was 7:20 AM. Like a high school student dreading that 8:00 AM first period class, I wasn't ready for another day of intense paddling on a surfboard to catch a ten-second wave (I know it's a "tough life" but lamenting is a trait I have perfected). I put on my bathing suit, finished breakfast and, in less than ten minutes, I was by the beach, ready for class. I was impressed by my efficiency. Just a few days before I needed more than thirty minutes to get ready for class, and, in fewer than a few days, I had managed to increase the time in bed and reduce morning preparations by twenty minutes. It was my fifth day and I had graduated to the advanced class, where I was going to paddle all the way out to catch the big waves.

My instructor introduced me to a young Australian blonde whose age I could not readily estimate. She was in the same bright-blue rash guard the school had given me. I was surprised given her non-athletic build that she was able to pick up the sport in just a few days, according to what Garcon, my instructor, had told me.

"Today is really crowded. No matter what direction I go in, I'm going to run into someone. Just look!" I said to Garcon as I pointed to the masses playing in the waves.

"Try not to hit them," he responded, clearly unmoved by my concerns.

So I abandoned my hesitations and went for the first wave I saw.

"PADDLE HARD! PADDLE HARD!" my instructor yelled from behind me.

I paddled harder just to get further from his yelling, as if I was swimming away from a shark. I rode the wave, jumped up, and felt like a pro. I was experiencing total freedom for a few seconds, with my mind suddenly cleared of concerns of what I would get for lunch, how dorky I looked in my helmet, or the strenuous paddling I needed to return to the waves when I finished. The mental noise was drowned out like a curtain pulled on a scene. It was only the wave, my board, and my body.

My trance-like bliss immediately shattered as the wave turned into a menacing wall of white water, and I noticed what I thought looked like a black bowling ball barreling toward me. However, it was too late to correct my position and I was aligned for a direct collision with the ball, which was transforming quickly into another surfer lying flat on her board. Before I could prepare myself, her board slammed into my shin and I fell, hitting my chin on a board on my way down.

"Are you okay?" she asked when I resurfaced.

"Yes, are you?"

She was fine.

"I didn't see you at all."

"I know that was my fault. I'm sorry."

And with that exchange everything seemed uneventful again. I paddled back out. As I recounted my close call to the other woman in my class, I ran my hand by my chin and felt a deep gash.

"Oh shit! I think I cut myself."

"Hold on. Let me look."

I stared at her, intently waiting for her assessment of my injury.

"Oh, it's not that bad," she said hesitantly, barely hiding her panic.

The instructor reacted similarly when he saw it but told me to catch one more wave. I couldn't tell if he wanted to distract me or if he thought it was no big deal.

I was the only one who couldn't see what had happened to me.

I made it back to the beach and asked the surf school photographer to snap a picture of me. He was confused until he saw what had happened below my chin. His face spoke the same alarm as the other three and, with worry, he urged me to go to the office. Obviously, anybody in my shoes would be feeling the degree of pain that was reflected in their expressions.

So with blood-soaked paper towels and a blood-stained rash guard, I went to the hospital. It was an intimidating feeling being driven to the hospital, especially on my own in a foreign country with no idea how bad the injury could be. I felt more alone perhaps than in any other situation. I felt no pain. Instead, panic, pain's father, set in and I lost control.

*How worried will Mom be? Will she worry and want me to come home?*

Suddenly, I felt weak and cold—even abandoned.

I remembered my friend Will, who had been diagnosed with cancer. He went through the same experience, but it was far more serious and grew worse every day of his remaining life. I thought of how courageous he had been—to not to give in and show fear when the expressions of all those around him were terrified after his unpredictable seizures; to know that he was destined for death and there was no way out of it; to keep up his spirit and the spirits of those around him when they were all crying, knowing there was no hope; to fight to survive when he was drifting in and out of life. How courageous he was to fight, knowing he was going to lose.

Those memories immediately stabilized my own mindset and squashed my fears. My epiphany had arisen courtesy of life experiences and the calling forth of the subconscious moments of serendipity they had instilled. I had put myself in this position. I wanted to test myself. I put the young woman there in my line of collision; I didn't allow myself to see her until the last second; I didn't allow myself to jump off the board backwards and miss the girl. I was here by a subconscious choice. Regaining my composure, I had nearly forgotten that I was being driven to the hospital.

At the hospital, others' facial expressions did not calm me and neither did the eighty or so people waiting in line. With a simultaneous sense of guilt and relief, I realized that, being a foreigner, I wouldn't have to wait in line or even get treatment in this forlorn-looking wing of the hospital. They took me to a much better-equipped wing with modern architecture and elevators where lines didn't exist. In fact, the doctor and nurse were waiting for me as if my life depended on their immediate attention. It didn't, of course. I received several stitches, and, fortunately, the injury looked worse than it was.

I never did see what happened, but I did get a glimpse of the magic that surrounds us each day and about which we're so often oblivious. It was a text message from the woman at the beach the day before who told me she would be texting on Saturday to remind me about church. It was ten in the morning on Friday and I had just returned from the hospital.

"Be of good COURAGE, and He shall strengthen your heart all ye that hope in the Lord. God always loves you and TRUST HIM. GOD BLESS YOU."

He was speaking directly to me and it couldn't have been more relevant.

Sitting in a surf office in Bali, I started bawling. Of all the messages she could send and all the passages she could pick, could I dare call this occurrence a fortuity? Could I brush it off as coincidence? To do so would be a lie and a lie to oneself is the worst possible kind.

Again, I was reminded of Milan Kundera:

"Though it might be wrong to chide one for being fascinated by mysterious coincidences, it is right to chide man for being blind to such coincidences in his daily life. For he thereby deprives his life of a dimension of beauty."

~

When I returned to the beach I sat down next to Gi, the young local renting out the lawn chairs and selling beverages. He was a young man in his mid-twenties with long hair showing nothing but his blonde highlights sticking out from under his Irish green baseball hat. He had the mellow attitude and aura of a surfer. For some reason, I became curious about his business.

"How many chairs do you rent a day?" I asked him.

"Maybe ten or fifteen . . . "

"How much do you make?"

"50,000 rupiah a day." (Roughly five dollars.)

It was then that the things came together for me. It was all clear.

"How would you like to go to Bluefin restaurant with me tonight?"

We had only known each other for a day and only really spoken superficially. Quick exchanges of hello and goodbye were the extent of our conversations.

"Blue-what?" he asked me.

"It's a nice sushi restaurant. I'll pay, of course."

"Sushi?" He looked at me, confused.

I explained to him that it was raw fish and he told me to call him before I go. So that night, I called him.

"I'm going in thirty minutes if you want to join me."

"Okay, I meet you. I go home and change."

Thirty minutes later, I met him in front of the hotel. He was still wearing his beach clothes.

"I cannot find my house key so I wearing same clothes. Maybe we can go and I will wait outside for you to eat." Gi suggested.

His humility was touching and almost brought me to tears. Here I was trying to be kind, while his statement, more natural than my efforts, eclipsed my intent five times over. His purity was effortless and second nature rather than a conscious effort. The most shocking part was that he actually had no obligation to me; he could have easily flaked out on me, a move some of my closest friends would not even hesitate to do. In many ways, I could consider this man a closer friend than most, a man willing to forego his own desires for another.

"No Gi, it's okay. They'll let you in."

This didn't reassure him; he seemed uncomfortable waltzing into tourist central.

"I've never been to a restaurant," Gi confessed to me at the last minute.

"Don't worry. We'll have fun. I'll meet you there."

I took a cab while he went to his brother's place to change clothes.

As we sat, the waitress put the dinner napkins on our laps. Puzzled, he looked up to the waitress for some explanation, but got none.

I ordered all kinds of sushi rolls, and when the food arrived, I saw that Gi had no idea what he was doing.

"Pick up your chopsticks," I told him as he struggled to hold them.

"Hold the back stick steady and push the front one back and forth." Before long he picked it up. I was surprised at how quickly he learned to eat with chopsticks. It took me several years to master them.

"What is this, Daria?" he asked, pointing to what appeared to him to be nothing more than various plates of uncooked fish and rice, obviously a scam in his book.

"Well, this one is yellowtail fish and this one is red tuna." He looked at me, nodding and pretending to understand.

"Before you start, put some wasabi on your tray and pour soy sauce on it. The more soy sauce, the less hot it will be."

His concoction was a chunk of wasabi and couple drops of soy sauce. Either my words were lost in translation or he enjoyed breathing fire. I gave him the benefit of the doubt as I didn't want to make him more nervous that he already was. He took a bite of his food after dipping it into his sauce. His tan face turned bright red, showing panic and shock for the first time. After a couple minutes, he mustered, "I don't like this one," pointing to his wasabi tray. I suggested he just use soy sauce without wasabi. During the course of the meal, he dragged his wrist along his mouth to wipe. But after watching me use the napkin, he followed suit. Eventually, his nerves settled and we were able to have a nice conversation. Like any two young guys, we began talking about the usual: girls, alcohol, and money.

"I went to the reggae bar last night and stayed late. This morning work was hard."

"How much is a beer there?" I asked curiously.

"Maybe 50,000 rupiah."

"So you spend a day's salary on one beer?"

"Yes, sometimes."

"How do you eat?"

"Well, I eat rice and egg every day for every meal for 3,000 rupiah." (Thirty cents.)

"If you go out, do you take the next day off?"

"Only two days off every month. I work too much . . . always tired. If very tired, my boss let me take day off," he explained to me.

My life at that moment was having every day off. I didn't wish to call myself lucky because I liked to think that, on some level, everyone chooses his or her reality and life. But at that moment, I appreciated my "choice" a little more than what I assumed Gi did with his.

"I don't like local girls," Gi told me. "I like foreign girls. I have two girlfriends in Sweden, one in Germany."

"So they live in different countries but they are your girlfriends?"

"Yes."

"So you never see them?"

"Yes, Lisa here two months before today."

"How about before that? When was the last time she came?"

"Two years before."

I couldn't help but laugh.

"That's not a girlfriend, that's just a girl you have fun with," I told Gi.

"Yes, yes . . . fun with." We both smiled at each other.

After dinner, Gi offered to drive me home on the back of his Vespa. He knew I was hesitant and so he gave me his helmet and said he would only drive through the side streets. It was frightening at first; the last thing I wanted was another trip to the hospital, but once I let go of the fear, it was exhilarating blasting through the narrow alleys and pedestrian streets, weaving through unsuspecting tourists. We said our goodbyes and called it a night.

~

A few days later, Gi asked if I wanted to go fishing with him. I had had my stitches removed earlier that day, which meant that I would resume surfing the next day. I immediately agreed to his offer.

At three in the afternoon, he picked me up on his Vespa and, this time, he had helmets for both of us. It was comforting knowing there was a sturdy plastic shell protecting my skull from the concrete we flew over at surprisingly quick speed. I was bigger and heavier than him and I could tell how difficult it was for him to maneuver with the added bulk on his scooter.

He pulled out onto a dirt road between two souvenir shops on the main road and eventually led me to a dirty pool. That's when I knew we weren't going deep sea fishing, or anywhere near the ocean. However, because I had never fished, the thought of catching fish was exciting no matter where we aimed to do it.

I was randomly hit with a wave of homesickness.

*What are you doing here, Dar? You should be in Sonoma with your family right now, on the waterslide, with Coco and Puff running around the pool, barking.*

I was distracted when Gi brought me a bag of live insects. I'm no entomologist but I knew it was a mix of pincher bugs and cockroaches, with stingers intact. I let Gi put them on the hook because I found it somewhat barbaric hooking live insects to the pole. I could see evidence of small-scale torture as they wiggled around, their thoraxes half pierced. I went with it and threw my hook into the pool. Within a couple of minutes I caught two catfish.

It wasn't long before Gi's whole family joined us, and I mean every imaginable relation—uncle and aunt, their kids, his parents, his brother, his cousin. They cheered me on, helping catch as many fish as possible. Every time I pulled in the reel and discovered a baby fish on my hook, the whole family, even the little four-year-olds, burst out laughing in triumph. Cooks in the shop, a humble hut, grilled and fried our fish and added rice and vegetables to the meal. I did not anticipate that the fish were intended for dinner on the spot so all of us sat cross-legged on a raised wooden platform by the ponds with a short table between us, packed with fish and side dishes.

"Gi, I've never eaten like this before," I confessed as I picked apart my unrecognizable fried catfish, trying to separate the bones.

"That's how I feel at restaurant."

I realized that he now watched me with the same enthusiasm I had when I observed him several nights before at the Bluefin restaurant. It was the same pure energy of sharing something new and exciting for the first time, in casual and candid fashion. Tonight, our roles had been reversed and I had been humbled with an important lesson.

The next day I was back surfing. We went to the reef, where the experience level was taken up quite a few notches. Now far from the tourist-filled beach, we were along a secluded coast where seriously advanced surfers tackled impressive barrel waves. The reef itself wasn't as scary as I thought it would be, despite it being quite shallow in certain areas (one bad fall in the reef and I'd have been back in the hospital), and there was about three times more paddling to be done here than before just to reach the waves.

After several failed attempts, I caught a perfect wave for my skill level and once again experienced a bona fide taste of surfing. As I collected my board and turned around, I came face to face with the pointed tip of a short board aimed at my head.

*Oh shit!*

I dove headfirst and barely escaped another major surfing injury. With satisfaction, I caught four waves in two and a half hours.

When I returned to the beach, I sat at Gi's table and found two Aussies in their forties or fifties sitting with six empty beer bottles in front of each of them, sipping on their next. During our conversation, I turned back to see a stunningly beautiful woman on the street looking over in our direction. I pointed her out to my new friends.

"Yeah, she's pretty. She's looking at you," the bigger Aussie told me.

"Really?"

"She ain't lookin' at us," the other Aussie chimed in.

She stood there for five minutes, and, then suddenly, a bird crapped right on my hand from the tree above us.

"That's good luck, you know," the bigger of the two guys said.

"I don't see how that's good luck. You got crapped on," the other one countered.

I turned back to see the woman, who had locked lips and tongues with her boyfriend, who apparently appeared out of nowhere. Talk about rubbing it in my face.

"Some luck," I said with resignation.

I left the guys to go for a dip and wash the crap off my hand. Refreshed and renewed, I saw Liana with two new people I had never met before: Natasha, a warm-hearted, outgoing younger woman from Jakarta, and her gay friend. They were naturally friendly and both worked at a five-star hotel.

"You haven't seen Dreamland? You haven't been up north?" the list went on as Natasha questioned me, quite taken aback how little of Bali I had experienced. There were so many things by tourist standards that I hadn't seen.

However, I was content to have fun just hanging out on Kuta beach every day. I didn't need to go to another beach because the sand was whiter or the water clearer. I didn't really agree with those who thought convention-ally that more fun could be experienced at a different spot—even though it's the same island, same coast, and same ocean. We're always afraid that we might miss some-thing so it might be prudent not to pass up the opportu-nity. Yet, the right thing could be precisely in front of us, even if we don't immediately recognize it because we're looking elsewhere for it.

"Natasha, how can you speak such great English?" I asked her, changing the subject, trying not to get too deep into the conversation.

"From Sesame Street. You know, Cookie Monster? My favorite character."

I couldn't stop laughing at her unexpected responses.

∾

My last day in Bali was upon me. I decided to enjoy my last day in paradise by the beach. In reality, every day of the journey thus far had been a form of paradise. I realized in my time to reflect that there were not enough happy people back home. Good energy is rare—a momentary occurrence rather than a daily certainty. Our lives suck out our energies the way we live at home, battling with everyone. We have to say no over several hundred times a day to stay on course. Something is wrong here—how do we get out?

During my last hours in Bali, I had a healer—or *reikki* master—work on me. In his calm and peaceful demeanor, he explained how he would open up my *chakras*, move the negative energy, and replace it with positive energy. After about five minutes lying on a massage bed with my eyes closed, I grew tired and transitioned into the deep state one goes into before falling asleep—except I didn't fall asleep, and instead stayed in that deep state. I could sense my thoughts, but they couldn't touch me—as if I watched this subconscious episode on television.

I awoke from that state and noticed it was dark outside. The session went for about ten more minutes before the *reikki* master, with the most gracious smile possible, instructed me to sit up. Obviously, not a single negative thought seemed to plague this man's mind, and for now, mine neither.

*Why do I have to leave tonight?*

I suddenly remembered Natasha was waiting at the beach. It was 7:30 PM and my flight was at 10:45 PM. I still needed to get dinner and Natasha was already in the restaurant when I arrived. She enjoyed hearing about my *reikki* experience.

"Don't you have to catch your flight soon?"

"I guess." My calm response triggered a reaction.

"What did this man do to you?"

One thing became acutely apparent in Bali. The locals seem so indebted to international tourists that one has the disturbing feeling of operating in a system that resembles some form of indentured servitude or, worse, economic slavery. By any reasonable measure, one must acknowledge that a person trying to sustain a livelihood on the mere equivalent of five American dollars a day is part of a highly flawed system.

I could feel the unspoken understanding of a shared struggle when observing two natives encounter each other in a restaurant, like Gi and the waitress at Bluefin. There was a humility that Gi felt knowing he was in that position by luck. In his case he was there because of me; in the other case, it was a young ingénue golddigging her way out of her situation. Either way, the only way out of their system is to latch on to a foreigner by any means. Imagine a nation—not a melting pot nation, nor a new nation—but one with natives whose blood lines can be traced thousands of years, and whose country's top amenities are reserved exclusively for the foreigners. It should not come as a surprise that resentment brews. But, in speaking to the Balinese locals, I saw nothing but purity and good intentions.

*How did they manage such selfless behavior?*

That might be the greatest secret of Bali . . .

~

# PART THREE

*Japan: Grace in Discipline*

~

## 12

Rushed and exhausted, I almost missed the critical leg of my marathon flight itinerary from Bali to Japan, but thanks to an alert airport staff member who found me passed out on a lounge bench, I made it. This would be an overnight flight into Darwin, then another to Cairns, and yet one more the next afternoon—it would take five hours to reach Tokyo. Of course, I also was facing two hours of train travel, including one shuttle in Tokyo. After being able to sleep ten hours a night in Bali, I was loopy after getting barely that much sleep the last two nights.

In Tokyo, I took the only train to Shinjuku. New, sleek, and spotless, the train impressed me in every way. It even had televisions in it. The ninety-minute trip, breezing through major districts of Tokyo, was as casual as a trip to the corner grocery store.

At the station, I was in a haze. I wasn't sure which exit to take, and who knew the Shinjuku station had a dozen different exits. I figured the southeast terrace path sounded like the best option. It was a bit scary. Here I was with no more than one hundred dollars in my pockets and a stuffed backpack, walking through unfamiliar streets, unable to speak the language, and unsure if a stranger would be willing to provide me accurate information should I need to ask. After Mongolia and Bali,

I thought that any travel anxieties would be nonexistent, but several frustrating attempts to hail a taxi and a complete unfamiliarity with this city lit up like the world's biggest rave proved otherwise. It was a whole different world yet again. I felt somewhat relieved when I did manage to get a taxi but when I arrived at the hotel, I immediately panicked when I reached into my pants pocket to discover it was empty. Quickly dispensing the possibility that I might have been pickpocketed, I recollected my thoughts and realized that the money was secure in my backpack.

It was 10:30 PM when I checked in at the hotel and, during an impulsive trip to check my email at the computer station in the lobby of the hotel, I met another adventurous backpacker, Johnnie, who was on the computer next to mine, getting his first-day bearings in Japan. We chatted a bit, latched on to each other, and decided to grab some dinner at a place he suggested. I decided to trust him. After all, he did have a twelve-hour head start on the Japanese experience.

It might have been late on a Wednesday evening but the streets were packed—without the chaos of an American megalopolis. I immediately noticed the chic, deceptively innocent Japanese women, including one with the motley yet fashionably smart ensemble of blue boots, a purple jacket, and a dress in black and pink. The vibrant colors were not limited to the LED billboards but extended to the wardrobes of every person walking the streets at eleven in the evening.

Johnnie was not a talker, so I didn't force the issue. Finally, we reached an alley after passing Hermes, Louis Vuitton, Tiffany, Armani, and Gucci—an avenue where one could blow an entire travel budget in minutes.

*I could just go on a spending splurge and end it all here.*

The thought tempted me for a few seconds before I got a hold of myself again and continued along.

The contrasts with the steppes of Mongolia, where one could see for scores upon scores of miles, struck me sharply. I was still in Asia, just a few hours east. Here, Johnnie was leading me like a native through a crammed maze into this narrow road packed with more people than I encountered during my entire two months in Mongolia. Tiny counters within the same walls were actually separate restaurants. We decided that the one that was nearly full would be the best choice and strode to the counter, hoping to secure two open seats. After one failed attempt, a couple of Japanese customers pulled out two other seats for us.

"Sit here," they told us in thick Japanese accents.

We sat and were immediately pelted with questions by these curious interrogators.

"From where? How long here?"

Likewise, we returned the favor.

"What should we eat?"

"Original ramen."

The man to my right was the most competent of all the people around us, all of whom were drunk and still in suits at 11:30 PM.

"What time you work 'til?" I asked, curious about the suits.

"Ten-thirty. Every night. Work many hard. Japanese always work. Then come drinking."

"Wow. You like your job?"

"No! Many stress! Always fighting! Always! Stress!"

Poor guy works all day and, with only enough time to sleep, still manages to get some beers in with the buds.

Now that I thought about it, it made sense why the streets were so crowded on a Wednesday night. They had all just left their offices.

"So what should I do here?"

His eyes glowed.

"First time?"

"Yes." (It wasn't, but I said yes anyway).

"Kabuki Cho! Very, very excite!"

His tone was definitely mischievous and I hesitated to probe him further.

He wrote on a piece of paper:

*Many woman = sex, many drinking . . . but very afraid.*

"Afraid?" I looked up at him.

He put his finger to his lips, silencing me and whispering while looking around.

"Japanese mafia! Many, many danger!"

He imitated a man who was drunk and stumbling, and acted out the part of another stealing his wallet.

"That's it? They take your wallet?"

I was expecting guns and knives to be involved.

"Yes . . . very afraid! . . . But very excite!"

Then, his drunken friend chimed in, yelling "Very excite!"

The man next to me smacked him in the head and said, "Sorry, my friend very drunk!"

I couldn't help but laugh. The man was so drunk he barely felt the slap. I wrote all of the places on a piece of paper as my new friend offered to pay and wouldn't take no for an answer.

"Here very cheap!" He argued when I pulled out my wallet.

"What's your name?" I asked him.

"Akio."

Akio kept insisting, though it came out to ten dollars per person (which for plain ramen isn't cheap in my opinion). He eventually paid and smacked his yelling friend hard on the head several times. The guy wouldn't get up. His arms were folded on the counter with his head buried between his arms. Akio and his coworkers dragged their friend out of the restaurant, not the lease bit concerned about whether he needed help or some water—more like "oh that, Shiguro, always getting drunk!"

Afterward, we joined our newfound friends on their journey to Kabuki Cho. Akio insisted on continuing to eat at a sushi bar, but the ramen had done its trick. I was too full and jetlagged to start an adventure in Kabuki Cho, no matter how "excite" it might have been. On our way back to the main street, a Nigerian man with a beige FUBU overcoat and a NY hat offered to "show us good girls." My new friend insisted, as politely as I've ever seen, "Maybe another time . . . thank you . . . very busy . . . thank you very much . . . so sorry . . . " with his palms pressed together, bowing deeply with each comment. It was the ultimate clash of cultures: the subtle and respectful versus the almost rudely blunt.

Before we split ways, my new Japanese friend gave me his card and said "trouble, call me" and left.

The next day I went to the Aikido world headquarters to get my membership card and general issue uniform, asking their permission to go to the Ibaraki *dojo*. Only after walking around lazily did I realize that Shinjuku, the part of Tokyo in which my hotel was located, was in the center of the city.

After easily obtaining permission from the headquarters, I decided to make the journey to Ibaraki the following day. I purchased a random ticket at an automated kiosk without a clue about whether it was the right fare but despite this, two hours later, I ended up in Iwama, a small town more than sixty miles east of Tokyo. The first taxi driver I hailed to take me to the Ibaraki *dojo* just pointed silently across the railway tracks. The town didn't appear too big and it seemed that crossing the tracks would be the largest fare he would get all day, yet he refused. Walking across the tracks, disoriented, I had no idea where to go; the lifeless roads gave no clues. At an empty convenience store, the employee gestured straight ahead and then right. I resumed this confusing search and just as I was approaching the town's outskirts, I spotted three others walking—a muscle-defined Burmese man, a much shorter and younger man, and a girl in a costume that I immediately recognized as Stitch from the film with Lilo.

"You looking for Ibaraki *dojo*?" the girl asked.

"Yes."

"Daria?"

"Yes."

"Welcome. We've been waiting for you. This is Keke and Win. My name is Sofia. I'm from Los Angeles. Where are you from?"

"San Francisco."

"Okay. The *sensei* told me you would be coming from the U.S. You have no Aikido experience?"

"No, I'm a total beginner."

"We've got another student who also just started a couple weeks ago: Francisco. You'll be staying with him. Now let's get you settled in."

The graveled grounds resembled a peaceful Zen garden, holding only two dilapidated wooden buildings surrounded by barren Japanese cherry blossom trees. The *dojo* mat we trained on served as our sleeping quarters at night with only the added benefit of a small futon and a bean-filled pillow. The kitchen seemed dark and humble, as if it hadn't been touched in years. Old packages of soy sauce lay strewn in different corners. Pots, pans, and heaters were tucked under dark wooden shelves and the refrigerator was to be shared by all. Apparently, we had to provide our own food.

When I unpacked my bags in a small changing room next to the *dojo* mat, I met Francisco, an awkwardly tall, skinny Portuguese guy about my age who had arrived two weeks prior. I was to have my first class that night. There were customs that Sofia explained to me before we stepped onto the mat.

"So you have to sit on your knees, and bow with your hands forming a triangle on the ground. Then the teacher will come in and you need to do it again, only this time he will say *"oneigeishimas"* and you say it back."

"I say what?"

"It sounds like '*oh my gosh, a mouse.*'"

"Is the class conducted in English?"

"No."

"So how do you understand what they are saying?"

"Well, I've picked up some Japanese, but you will just have to watch and your partner will explain it to you."

Everyone sat in class, stretching and chatting until the *sensei* arrived. The air quickly became tense and serious, the chatter ending abruptly. The students formed a line and I continued to sit.

"You need to sit at the end of the line," Sofia whispered, annoyed at my inexperience. The teacher and everyone looked on in impatience.

*Great way to start, Dar.*

The *sensei* turned and faced away from us, bowing to a statue of O'Sensei, the founder of Aikido, as everyone followed suit. He then held his hands out and clapped twice with the class. He then faced the class and bowed again in unison with the class.

"*Oneigeishimas!*" he yelled forebodingly.

"*Oneigeishimas!*" the class responded, Sofia's voice screaming above the others.

I quickly determined she would be the teacher's pet for my time here, potentially making my life miserable. The *sensei* quickly went through the first exercise while the class watched attentively. He spoke very little during the demonstration and we were off. Everyone jumped up, quickly picking their partners. Sofia and Francisco avoided my gaze.

I was the pledge.

After the first exercise, we sat in *seiza* (sitting on the knees with the top of the feet flat on the ground). The rough mat uncomfortably dug into my soft skin, leaving me in pain while the *sensei* elaborately demonstrated the next move. It looked more like a dramatic acrobatic exhibition as the student somersaulted in the air while the *sensei* bent his hand in a certain direction. Matching up with a partner who practiced the move just demonstrated, I realized the reason he flipped during the demonstration was to prevent a broken wrist. Here I was with my arm twisted in the same position, wishing I could flip but extremely afraid I'd break my back in order to avoid injuring my wrist.

After a grueling class of constant pain from relentlessly twisted limbs, which to my surprise had lasted just an hour, one of the *senseis* joined us for dinner. Win, the muscular Burmese who greeted me earlier, cooked eggs and lettuce for us, a welcome delicacy with sake to take it down. Arthur and Dominic, colleagues in this collective torture as *uchideshi*, joined us for dinner as well. All the *uchideshi*, or live-in students, were about my age except Win who, though he looked about twenty-eight, was actually forty-two, and Sofia, who was nearing her forties. Retiring for the night, I confronted the same quarter-inch-thick mat I had just practiced on. I laid my futon atop the *dojo* mat—which might as well have been hardwood floor—and slept like a baby.

I awoke at dawn to the sound of stomping feet scuffling and scrambling to leave the *dojo*. Half dazed, I made out Francisco's tall figure and followed after him, collecting and stacking my stuff in an absent-minded rush. Outside, the other *uchideshi* came from many different directions—the Australian, the Burmese, the Polish, and Portuguese. The *sensei* was an old dark-skinned man whose wrinkles likely came from too much time in the sun. For a man who appeared to be in his late sixties or early seventies, he walked firmly. He waited in the car as Keke and Win jumped in and left.

"So can we go back to sleep?" I asked daringly as the *sensei* drove off.

Dominic laughed and said flatly, "no." At twenty-five, he was a second-degree black belt from Australia who arrived in Ibaraki much in the same way a Muslim goes to Mecca—to pay homage to the shrine of Aikido. He was a lanky boy off the mat but in action, he had tremendous confidence and ability, capped by a rich sense of humor and endless supply of witty remarks.

We were handed rakes to clean the sandy garden of the leaves. All the rake marks were to go in a specified direction. Once finished, Francisco showed me the art of cleaning the toilets.

"Isoyama shihan is coming today!" Sofia warned me. "He's the headmaster of this *dojo*. I've only had one class with him and I've been here a year. You should consider yourself extremely lucky."

"Why?" I asked naively.

"He has one of the highest degrees in Aikido, and he taught Steven Segal."

He arrived several hours later. The *uchideshi* gathered around him like children around a teacher, waiting for a moment of wisdom to be imparted.

"Where is the new student?"

Sofia pointed towards me as I stumbled out of the changing room, struggling to put my shoes on. He looked towards me in contempt and continued walking with the others towards the *dojo*. We prepared for class, the air even thicker with tension than the night before. As we prepared for class he interrogated me publicly.

"Why are you here?" he said in a piercing tone.

"Well, um . . . I read a little about Aikido and its philosophy seemed in line with what I believe."

I was impressed with my impromptu response, but Isoyama shihan didn't buy it. I wasn't entirely sure that he understood what I had said either.

"Stand up," he ordered.

I stood in front of the class.

"Who taught you to tie your belt?"

I was frozen and confused.

"No one."

"Win, you need to teach Daria how to tie his belt properly. You are not leading by example." He went on to reprimand in Japanese.

Win bowed his head, accepting full responsibility.

After some research, I discovered that Ibaraki is Aikido's second most important *dojo*, where students train to become *sensei*. Now, I wished for the benefit of some previous experience to fully appreciate this *dojo*. I knew I was in over my head.

## 13

The following day, there were new faces: Juan, a young man from Mexico, and Mille, a fifty-two-year-old Italian who left his family for a month to improve his Aikido. "In Italy we make a break time between techniques to make a joke and look at girls," he said, sounding like Borat. "Now I want more serious environment."

Francisco, Juan, Mille, and I headed to Uchihara, a nearby town with a big mall, the next day. It was a national holiday so there was no scheduled training. We looked through the shops but Fran and I split from the others to eat sushi. When our food arrived there was a red triangular piece of paper in my plate but no napkin. We ate while we tried to figure out the significance of this small paper triangle.

We asked for the bill and the server asked for the red paper, which apparently contained a message in the fold. The guy lit up and left the table, only to return carrying a twelve-pound bag of rice that he placed in my arms. It was a prize I had won, kind of like when McDonald's offers Monopoly stickers on their packages of fries. The prize was more of an annoyance as I awkwardly carried it around the mall with me.

≈

We woke up late again the next morning. It was 5:30 AM and temperatures had dipped below freezing. The grass was speckled with frozen dew and I was regretting shaving my hair the night before. I had become a popsicle. We dressed in the standard martial arts uniform: traditional white pants and Gi top (though mine was the only cream-colored uniform). We tied belts around our waists and picked up our *bokken* and practiced our swings with the wooden swords. Everyone counted aloud in Japanese, even Francisco, who had been there for only two weeks. Lost for words and needing to improvise, I began to count in Farsi when it was my turn (*"Yek! Do! Seh!"*)—which struck me as memorably peculiar in this remote outpost deep inside Japan.

We continued to practice our swings, coming down on car tires and aiming to keep our *bokken* firm despite its bounciness. Finally, it was time for knuckle pushups on the concrete. Not knowing any Japanese, I lost track of the rep count, which apparently was a blessing. After practice we ate, and Juan, emboldened by my embrace of the chrome dome look, shaved his head, too.

∿

The following day was brutal; my homesickness seemed to aggravate the negative tone of the day. We practiced in the morning as usual until we split into groups of two. The *sensei* commanded something in Japanese and I looked on, confused, as half the group walked off the mat. They returned with solid wooden blocks wrapped in thick ropes. Keke, my partner, held one out in front of me.

"What is this?" I whispered.

"You have to punch," he managed in his broken English.

"*Ich!*" the sensei screamed in an uncharacteristic tone as everyone dug knuckles into the ropes.

"*Ni!*"

His voice emanated such a contagious strength that the louder he yelled, the bolder I was willing to punch the unforgiving wooden block. We had several rounds of this before I witnessed the horror scene that was my knuckles. Blood covered the better part them, and my soft skin was lacerated by the thick ropes.

We topped off the morning class with *ukemes* (standing flips) and it only took two attempts before my back ached in more places than I could count. None of it really phased me much, though. At the *dojo*, one learns to deal with all of the numerous discomforts; there is no other choice. Even if I did want to complain, most of the teachers wouldn't understand what I was saying anyway.

The construction of the *dojo* would make an HGTV host cringe. Insulation was a novel concept here and the doors had gaps one could fit a small baby through. Use of the space heaters was strictly prohibited as per *sensei's* orders.

During breakfast, Dominic asked me what sports I played and when I mentioned tennis Sofia interrupted, "A real rich kid's sport."

I ignored the remark and when Dom asked me what my job was back home, she jumped in again: "Ask him what his father does—not him."

Once again, I ignored her retort, but decided to press the issue when she added, "At the university of spoiled children all you get are immature boys."

"How many people do you know with a well-rooted career at the age of twenty-two?" I said.

"I had one. I planted trees in the Dominican Republic," she said. Sofia was now forty and had been here at the *dojo* for a year; she knew the routine quite well and had given herself the role of *dojo* manager. I had no idea why she was after me. And it didn't end there. Later that day, one of the *senseis* showed up and, because I was snoozing away with my headphones on, I didn't appear for the customary bow. Belatedly, I found out and joined the group.

"Where were you when the *sensei* showed up?" she snapped.

"I didn't hear him, I was listening to music."

"Well, listen with one ear plug," she said curtly, like an angry parent.

"Was *sensei* mad?"

"No, he didn't notice. But I don't care. You need to be here."

The idea of constantly being on alert drained me. Sofia blamed me for not putting away my dry dishes— which I did—the dishes in question belonged to someone else. She was annoyed that there was plastic in the compost bin and made me clean it even though I hadn't been the careless one. No one helped. I watched those who left dinner early escape without cleaning their plates. I told her of this predicament.

Sofia was unmoved. "You don't know what other work they do. You do what you can here."

For some, apparently, that was nothing.

Sofia was merely an annoying fraternity pledgemaster. I had initially thought about staying two months at the *dojo*, but I was now contemplating leaving the next day. The nostalgic feelings of a loving family, my pets, Coco and Puff, and securely insulated surroundings complete with heated toilet seats tempted me. Here, in the cold and damp *dojo*, people either fascinated me or left me with deeply detestable feelings. Even the *sensei*'s bragging about his new Toyota irked me.

But I was stuck here with this schedule by my own resolve, forced to adhere to the code of conduct and accept whatever Sofia threw at me.

Reality smacked me back to humility as I remembered the real reason for this journey. The coldness of the surroundings—with temperatures no more than five degrees celsius outside and a starkly barren chamber with no insulation or lighting—were amplified by the raw unwelcoming behaviors of a few individuals. These things made my decision to stay that much more difficult.

There were only two warm spots here: directly under the hot shower water (which actually was more torturous because of the anticipation of stepping out into the unforgiving cold once again), and in my sleeping bag. So, naturally, I tried to take naps often and go to sleep early. But after my nap, it was time for evening *keiko*, which meant the uncomfortable feeling of releasing all the heat I had stored up in my sleeping bag all day. I changed into my uniform and went on the mat for class. Before we started class, an elder black belt ordered us to remove all the wooden panels, the only protection from the arctic-like breezes.

"Why don't we open the windows, too? It's so hot in here!" I suggested to Francisco and Mille, who were sitting next to me. As I tried to stretch out my hamstrings, my freezing muscles clenched up, unwilling to loosen up in time for class.

The hour-long class was a dreadful experience. With sore knees, I changed into civilian clothes and headed to the kitchen for dinner, glad to have finished another night of torture. I had put on four more layers than I had on during class, but I was still cold.

Meanwhile, the Europeans were dropping like flies. Francisco had contracted cold-like symptoms with a fever and a headache; Mille had a stuffy nose and was managing headaches for the past four days; and our newest member, Nikki from Austria, felt ill as well. I decided to eat some cereal and get out of there and into the warm sleeping bag as quickly as possible.

It was just 9:30 PM and sleep was the sole pleasure to be had until Win's 4:50 AM wakeup call the next morning. He was generous in letting us sleep until six, but not generous enough to allow us to skip morning *keiko* due to the harsh weather conditions. The temperature was at freezing and again we had to change into our uniforms. The few rays of light emanating from the sun did provide the slightest modicum of warmth and a reason to be a little more grateful. If that didn't warm us up, perhaps the 2,500 bokken swings helped, followed by the 150 pushups and other Aikido-related body building exercises.

Our individual resilience was put to the test because we all had the option to leave at any time. It was harder for me because, as a beginner, my body wasn't accustomed to getting my arms and joints twisted in extreme movements, nor was it used to the *ukemes* required in order to avoid a break or fracture. I hadn't come here to perfect my Aikido skills like the others. However, my reasons for being here were deeper than a desire to hone skills. Mine was a personal mission of strength, empowerment, and understanding.

One of the most difficult things was wrestling myself away from the notion that learning a skill required a specific purpose to be attached to it. At times, vague answers to practical questions were the best I could expect: "You are not supposed to get in that situation," or "Aikido is not fighting," or "You must dodge the punch," or "You shouldn't ask these kinds of questions." If martial arts were a form of self-defense, then why were questions about its practicality considered illegitimate? It turned out I still had a lot to learn.

Japanese teaching differed in every possible way from my martial arts training in the U.S. Though I didn't have any Aikido experience, I did have Jiu-Jitsu and kickboxing experience. Our *sensei* taught in Japanese and most times they didn't even say anything—they merely demonstrated the technique twice and let the student struggle. Well, at least I struggled. I knew the techniques were hard when I saw the black belts struggling as well. However, once someone thought that he or she had unlocked the key to comprehending the significance of what the *sensei* had demonstrated, there was the equally frustrating and humbling challenge of mastering the next technique. In this manner, Aikido kept us honest and shattered any ego that we managed to cultivate through the slightest understanding of a technique.

Frustration with the art was countered by the profound sense of peace it brought to those practicing it. It was simply a disguised form of meditation—much like surfing in Bali. Gone were the ordinary concerns of the day or of life in general. Forget thinking about the past or the future or about what sounds good for dinner. Nothing mattered. It took me there without me noticing it, because if I noticed, I wouldn't have been there, and that was the beautiful anarchy of being in the zone. The metaphor of sweeping our mind clean as we swept the leaves away in the Zen garden strikes me as appropriate. Surprisingly, I was always in high spirits after cleaning and *keiko* in the morning.

The others around me also emerge as examples of life's potential goodness. The *uchideshi* developed into my new family, a band of brothers. We became inextricably linked through our shared experience at the *dojo*. Once one is accepted by the long-term *uchideshi*, the individual becomes a part of the *dojo* regardless of the *sensei's* personal assessment. *Uchideshi*—not the *sensei*—run the *dojo*.

My journey was far from complete, and who knew what India and Nepal would bring. My perspective was only just beginning to open and broaden. The most basic level of perspective obviously came in the social and cultural differences I saw in the countries I was visiting. However, deeper than that was my inner perspective, which integrates these external experiences. At its core, perspective portends to reveal our most surprising truths. For example, my surfing accident first seemed like a bad situation, but once I started to see myself not as the victim but as the creator of a test for myself, I was able to relax and accept the circumstances for what they were. I had fashioned my testable hypothesis: if your perspective determines your experience of life, then you can have whatever experience you choose by changing your perspective. This means letting go of victimhood. Whatever frustrations I was experiencing were transitory and necessary for my growth; my ability to cope with them, overcome them, and move along until the next set of frustrations proved invaluable. In theory, one can continuously change his or her perspective on events so that he or she feels the way they want to feel about everything. Our life lies so completely in our perspective.

Francisco, the last of the short-term *uchideshi*, left the *dojo* with a goodbye party. It was strange being the only one sleeping in the *dojo*, as all the long-term *uchideshi* got their own rooms. I felt alone in my dreams and woke up to no one next to me. I slept with all my clothes, including my jacket, and was still cold. In the morning it was minus one degree celsius. *Keiko* was brutal. The frost numbed my toes. Concerned about frostbite, I put on my ski socks and still barely felt my feet ten minutes later. The water in the toilet froze along with the pipes, so we couldn't wash our hands. This was the coldest day so far.

Despite the cold, I was reminded of perspective once again. Two brothers—one a devout Kevintian and the other an atheist—share the experience of watching a sibling die. The devout looks at the death with complete faith, knowing that God has taken this sibling to a better place. Thus, he has an easier time coping and regrouping. In fact, his faith is so fortified that he sees the event as purely good—a well-earned respite. On the other hand, the atheist curses, victimizing himself and wondering why this had to occur. He sees himself as a victim of external negative events and cannot cope with the situation.

Faith is simply a means of perspective change, and an extremely strong one at that. Faith in its purest form is a miracle. Therefore, we can confidently conclude that perspective is the only reality we have. There is no ultimate reality for us. Unlike the idea of two sides—positive and negative—to every argument, in life, there can also be two—make that, many—perspectives for every event.

With each day in my travels, I became more firmly convinced that in the Western world, consumerism and incessant accumulation are our only perspectives.

~

John, my best friend back home, confirmed his forthcoming weeklong ski excursion to Japan. I had been gone four months without seeing a longtime friend, and I was a bit surprised by how much I missed that contact. I had second thoughts about staying longer in Iwama because I could see significant improvement in my daily exercise. The cold early mornings, however, loomed over my head like impending death. That did it. I pursued an alternative plan of visiting Aki, an Aikido teacher I had met at a ceremony held for the founder of Aikido. The plan was to stay at her house for two weeks before heading onto Nagano to ski with John.

~

As my departure date neared, I vacillated about coming back to Iwama during the coldest part of the winter, after my ski vacation. It wasn't about rank as much as a sense of personal fulfillment. If I didn't return, I would risk losing most of what I had learned there because the foundation I was building had yet to reach its critical stage. I decided to leave my return open-ended. After all, two more months could be tolerated with ease. On the other hand, that would have meant being abroad for more than a year, well beyond the threshold my family and friends were willing to handle back home.

At the age of twenty-two, I was well past the age when I could take the time to experience life rather aimlessly. I'm not sure at what point that time began and ended, but I knew it had expired. The time, at least for me, was past due for record-breaking life accomplishments. I guess I somehow missed the train of allowable enjoyment somewhere between SATs and finishing college. Any time one allocates to himself for such global experiences is considered a waste of time by some, but the progressive bounds I was making in psychological development were immeasurable.

I had to admit that, thanks to popular culture and media exposure, this sort of self-discovery process had become stereotyped or even cliché, especially as it pertained to the peers of my generation. The notion of "Oh, he wants to go find himself" carried mixed and mostly negative connotations. Perhaps the guy was confused, crazy, or momentarily lost. But, as Socrates so wisely stated, "Wisest is he who knows he does not know."

## ⮜ 16 ⮞

As I prepared for my departure from Iwama, memories of my stay in the cold *dojo* came flooding back. The day before yet another ceremony, this one honoring the Doshu, we rode bikes to a nearby small town to buy cheap suits that we would wear for the occasion. We stopped at a used goods store that was arranged like an obstacle course, with futons and coat racks we had to climb over to reach the used suits. The coats were around twenty dollars and either too small or just ugly. We were all confused about what to do, so we did what any confused foreigner in Japan would do—eat sushi.

The next day's ceremony was long and boring but the banquet afterward was unforgettable. I sat with three women, Juan, Mille, and Toshihiro *sensei*. Much to Toshihiro *sensei's* dismay, the women poured drinks and fed me before the rest, and they ensured I had more than my share. *Sensei* wanted them to eat before the students but the women would have it no other way. My charm paid off as I was literally starving from the day's work and activities. Meanwhile, Francisco was placed at a table where the *senseis* didn't leave much for the others. I even managed a photo with the great Doshu. After the banquet we went back to the *dojo*. At this point the sun was low and it felt like 8:00 PM but it was only 2:00 PM.

The festivities continued, with a much smaller group, at the *dojo*. Every *uchideshi* had to make a speech. It was my turn. I stood and let my feelings take over.

"I am here from San Francisco. I am backpacking around the world and have spent the last three months in Bali and Mongolia. When I got here, I knew nothing about Aikido. However, in the last month I have realized how deep this art goes. It is more than just martial arts; it is a culture, a history, and a way of life. The people I have been living with have become like my brothers and sisters and I would welcome them with open arms if they ever came to San Francisco. The *senseis* here are kind and yet they have a strength about them that is admirable. Japanese people are so kind and at times I wish I were Japanese. There is a discipline here that is unrivaled in my experience, and a meticulous attention to detail. This will be a step I will never forget."

The speech was well received, even by the *senseis*. Even Sofia complimented me on my speech. Isoyama *sensei* asked a few questions to clear up any words he didn't quite pick up and then looked on at me with approval when I sat.

I went to bed before the rest of the *uchideshi* that night and woke up to the grunts of the Polish *sensei*.

*Is this guy practicing his moves, drunk at midnight?*

I ignored it, continuing to sleep. His grunts left my curiosity no choice but to turn over to shut him up, but I saw that he was puking, with another *uchideshi* patting his back. They made Juan clean it as they thought I was asleep. I was no longer the only one to have thrown up on the mat. It had become a rite of passage.

～

Despite my occasional gripes with the *senseis*, I was forever indebted for the moments of enlightenment and empowerment they had allowed me to experience, even if there were some inadvertent *faux pas* moments. One day, we had three *keiko* (training) sessions scheduled. The morning session involved timed segments of wooden sword fighting and I was highly anticipating the 10:00 AM session with Shihan. I was a little apprehensive because Shihan's class focused on the minor technicalities that he believed black belts forget or become lazy and complacent about and didn't help much for someone who barely even understood the basics.

In class, Shihan watched me intently. Finally, he interrupted my partner and me to explain the concepts I lacked and I stood there, nodding and listening. Afterward, he turned to Keke and said, "You need to teach Daria some respect."

I was in shock.

*Have I been disrespectful? What did I miss?*

I had no idea what he was talking about. It was only later that Keke explained, for the first time, that I was supposed to take a step back and kneel when being instructed, as if I were being knighted.

Another memorable class occurred one evening when it was unusually full. We had ten extra Polish students, ten *uchideshi*, and about a half dozen people who were from Iwama and attending evening keiko. Add the two *senseis*, and we had nearly thirty people on mats in a space normally full with between ten and fifteen students. There was no room to fall or really practice comfortably. On top of it all, I was frustrated because I wasn't understanding the techniques and not a single teacher cared to help. I was eventually partnered with Mille, who also was a white belt like me. We were given six techniques to practice in succession, but unfortunately I understood only one of them. Mille, not so surprisingly, only understood the same one, too. We looked at each other, laughing in our collective frustration about our situation. Everyone in this zoo of a class knew what to do except us. I was growing increasingly upset at the situation when suddenly a thought popped into my head:

*I am paying seventy-five cents for this! And complaining!*

In the U.S. you can't even pay seventy-five cents for a pack of gum, let alone a class with some of the premier Aikido instructors and students in the world! I couldn't help but laugh at my ludicrous frustration. If anything the exposure alone was worth the price. So I squashed my anger and did the best I could. I resolved never to complain about lack of attention again.

The time had finally arrived to leave Iwama and I packed my bag, a little heavier with the winter jackets my parents had sent to get me through the blistering cold of the *dojo*. Traveling by train had become a keenly anticipated pleasure in Japan. There was never any uncertainty about making the correct station transfers.

Aki awaited me at the Yokohama station. After seeing her house, I couldn't help but feel relieved to finally be in a "true" house again after five months. The warmth and coziness of the house was a feeling I had managed to forget. The house, however, was in need of some attention: old untouched papers were stacked on the kitchen counter, expired batteries littered the table strewn with half a dozen remotes (none of which worked), and the hallway was full of old electronic equipment that had been abandoned and never thrown out. As I walked up the second set of stairs to what would be my room, I came across boxes of old clothes and music notes. My room, in the attic, was stacked with bookshelves and books on topics from Buddhism to the Cold War. The house had been neglected for some time.

Judging from her hectic schedule, it seemed that Aki was trying to keep herself busy to distract herself from the fact that her house no longer felt like her home anymore. I was given a bed, a pillow, a soft mattress, and a room with a heater—luxuries I had not had since leaving California. The smallest things made a big difference.

At the outset Aki seemed calm and confident, but the more I spoke to her the more I realized how lonely she was as a Japanese divorcee living alone in Yokohama. At the age of sixty, she was still as fit as a personal trainer. She didn't carry the excess belly fat that plagued most Americans. Instead, years of Aikido practice had kept her body toned and nimble. Only the few wrinkles on her face gave away the pain she had endured, but she told me that the way she saw it, she finally had the opportunity to do all the things she'd always wanted to do. Her optimism was inspiring.

The next morning, I woke at 6:00 AM and chuckled, thinking that my fellow *uchideshi* had already awakened an hour earlier to rake the leaves outside the shrine. Meanwhile, I fell back asleep and woke at ten. We headed straight to Aki's *dojo* to train.

Aki later went to pick up her eighty-seven-year-old mother. She walked into the house slowly, carrying not only a cane but also the biggest smile I had ever seen. It warmed my heart to see this woman; her spectacles and white hair completed the picture of the cutest grandmother I had ever seen. I went to the grocery store and bought the ingredients to make spaghetti and spent some time cleaning and organizing Aki's fridge. As I dug into the fridge, I realized that I was digging into the depths of the neglect this house had seen. I pulled out rotten vegetables, canned food and cheese that had expired years prior, and leftovers in Tupperware that I didn't dare open. One third of the items in the fridge were immediately thrown in the garbage. To make matters worse, a can of Coke spilled, making everything sticky. The process took well over two hours and I didn't even get to the freezer.

Aki called me a bit later.

"Can you help me with some shopping at Costco?"

"Sure."

"Come outside in ten minutes. I have some good news for you, too."

It had to be a girl. What else could it be? I was excited for my assumed encounter with whatever woman Aki had in mind.

When Aki arrived, however, I was disappointed to find an old man (a neighbor) in the car.

"Daria, this is my neighbor."

I hoped he wasn't the surprise, but I didn't ask. We quickly dropped him off a couple blocks later and Aki confirmed my suspicion.

There was a girl in my near future.

And just as quickly as we dropped off the old man, we picked up two young Japanese women. They seemed to be right around my age, half Japanese, and they could speak fluent English. I was instantly attracted to Mari, who had long light brown hair, a silky soft white face, and the most uncharacteristic freckles on her round cheeks. Her stylish red blouse and fashionable coat contrasted sharply with the jeans and jacket I had been wearing for the last couple months. She was the epitome of femininity and clearly had paid more attention to her outfit than I ever did to my college applications. Even the ribbons on her shoes matched the color of her blouse.

If only she knew that I wasn't a bum and that I had chosen this lifestyle. I felt like Aladdin wanting to impress Jasmine. The other girl, Liz, was more modest, obviously less interested in her wardrobe, and interested instead in intellectualizing. She dressed very much like an American with a plain t-shirt and jeans. Her glasses matched her personality. She was getting her masters in England and spoke in a sophisticated English accent about neuroscience.

"We made a recent discovery about the brain's particular link with the body and the subconscious power of the mind." She went on for several minutes.

"Guess why Daria is here." Aki interrupted, to my relief.

"What?" Mari asked in a curious tone.

Realizing that Aki just wanted to give me a chance to speak more than anything, I jumped right into it.

"Well, I've been traveling around Asia to learn about specific cultural practices to strengthen my understanding of Eastern religion and spirituality."

That was it. They were hooked. I continued on about my plans for India and Nepal, and my experiences in Mongolia, Bali, and Japan—which blew them away. It was unfair. I had caught them off guard as I'm sure neither woman expected a young, attractive man traveling across the world in search of spiritual strength through rigorous activities—let alone one who would be staying with Aki in that part of Japan. They were both at a loss for words, so they pulled out the familiar "I have a boyfriend" tactic. That's when I knew the game tilted in my favor. Their strategy to make themselves appear unattainable, to give themselves an edge, to make me jealous, was evident. But their blushing cheeks told it all. Everyone at the age of twenty-two knows what a boyfriend or girlfriend really means: nothing serious. I continued my story with a huge smile across my face.

After our shopping escapade, we dropped off Liz and were close to Mari's house. I was in a bind—how to keep Mari from going home?

"You should join us for dinner!" I blurted.

"Yeah. I don't think you have any plans; your mom is out tonight," Aki said, her response distinctly helpful.

"Well, I have some work to do and I bought a hot dog from Costco."

"Oh, come on, it's Christmas Eve and I'm making pasta. There is no way you are eating that hot dog."

Though we weren't planning on celebrating Christmas Eve, I thought it would be a compelling reason for her to come nonetheless. Though the Japanese do not celebrate Christmas, the streets were lit up with Christmas lights and the city felt festive. Aki was planning her own Christmas party the next day.

"Well, let me feed my parrot."

While we waited in the car for Mari, Aki gave a little more background about our guest.

"I know her mom. She is a pianist with a Ph.D. from Yale and her dad went to Harvard. She has her own TV show here."

I realized I wasn't the only one with an impressive resume.

I prepared spaghetti and garlic bread for the three women: Aki, her mother, and Mari. We cooked, drank wine, and spoke about music.

"So Aki tells me you're on TV?"

"Yes. Well I have a radio show I host for Fox. I actually had a Christmas song I sang when I was little that made me a little celebrity. But the video is embarrassing."

"Oh, come on, you know you have to show me now."

She quickly located her video on YouTube, and there was baby Mari singing *Last Christmas*. Her song was in the Top 10 on the Japanese Billboard charts.

The spaghetti turned out fantastic, which impressed my dinner companions. After the meal, I booted up my laptop to show them photos of my trip and life in the U.S. Aki's grandmother sat with me the whole time, watching every image. She finally told Aki something in Japanese and Aki and Mari burst out laughing.

"What did she say?" I asked with a first grader's impatience.

"She wants to give you a photo of herself."

I couldn't help but laugh either.

"I'd love one!"

"You know, Daria, you really should meet my daughter, Julie," Aki said.

I immediately looked to catch Mari's reaction. Right on cue, she stood silently, pretending to be detached.

Mari volunteered to show me around the city after dinner, so we grabbed our jackets and headed to the nearest 7-11 for wine.

"Do you think they have a bottle opener?" I asked her.

"The bottle is probably a twist-off top. It's 7-11. I'm sure they don't expect people to buy good wine here. It's made for convenience."

She was right.

We walked the streets, festooned with Christmas lights all the way to downtown Yokohama. The city was breathtaking, rivaling the Embarcadero in San Francisco: a beautiful city by the bay lined with skyscrapers. We found the first bar—looking more like a restaurant and, at best, half a respectable establishment at that—that we could to get out of the cold and warm ourselves with more liquor. The place had a vibe like the Boston hangout on *Cheers* but the big difference here was that this one had a top-of-the-line Toto bidet. After ten minutes of waiting in an empty bar for a drink, we grew impatient.

"You want to just leave?" I asked Mari.

"I don't know, I think they might be bringing it."

I looked over at the empty restaurant.

"There's no one here and they haven't brought us the drinks yet. I think they don't deserve our business. Let's go to a bar where they will actually give us a drink."

Dashing before our order arrived, we took a cab to Aki's house and found a couple bars willing to serve us on Christmas Eve. We were the only ones bar hopping around the streets of Yokohama.

Once our spirits were high, we headed home.

"Do you have that one song, Apologize by One Republic?" I asked Mari on a drunken whim.

"Of course! I love that song."

My spirit was doing inner somersaults at her answer. She pulled out her iPhone and started to play it.

*I'm holding on your rope got me ten feet off the ground.*

As she swayed her hips to the music, I pulled her closer to me. She slowed to my pace as we began rocking in sync and getting more comfortable with each other's touch. We glanced at each other—her eyes open, vulnerable, innocent. My lips were drawn to hers as the whole day was expressed in a simple kissing gesture. Her lips trembled tenderly, her body bending to accommodate mine. It was an ethereal experience of sensual tension unleashing itself in this empty street. We were on center stage, kissing passionately, like lovers. It was the purest most unexpected joy of my trip so far.

~

I waited impatiently the next day for Mari to show up at Aki's Christmas party. I constantly kept an eye by the door throughout every conversation, hoping that she was just stuck in traffic. There was no traffic on Christmas day in Yokohama but I was hoping for a holiday miracle. The night dragged on slowly as I finally accepted the fact that she probably would not be attending.

I had been drinking on all four days I had been with Aki and this day would be no exception, thanks to the year-end *bonenkai* celebration with her swordsmanship class. There was no shortage of sake and Asahi as we drank to let go of sorrows and past troubles. The *sensei* sat near me, asking questions about my Aikido experience throughout lunch, while he continuously poured me more beer and sake. Once again, I was hammered.

Aki's phone rang and after seeing the caller ID, she looked at me with a big smile. It must have been Mari. The adrenaline rushed through my body, my heart pounding to hear what she had to say. Aki finished up the conversation and looked over to me.

"Well, what did she say?" I asked impatiently.

"It wasn't Mari. It was Liz. She wants to pick up her scarf from my house."

# ⌖ 18 ⌖

The next morning, Aki and I packed early to head to her beach house in Shimoda. Though the drive took us about five hours, the narrow roads nestled in the hillside along the vast Pacific were a breathtaking distraction. I never really thought of Japan as a country filled with scenic coasts. I had always imagined the nation as the land of Tokyo, the concrete jungle, sushi and Akihabara, the mecca of electronics, shrines, and monasteries. Little did I know that this side of the Pacific Ocean offered unforgettable coastlines with crystal clear and warm water, even in January. We came upon various small empty beach towns and pulled into a small shopping center for sushi. We sat at the traditional counter with the typical sushi conveyor belt offering all sorts of fresh fish and advertising certain combination platters with bold Japanese characters.

Aki's beach house, set high in the hillside, was a relaxing getaway from the busy streets of Yokohama. Here she had no more than three other neighbors on her street, and the mood was tranquil. Still exhausted from the recent celebrations, we kept it simple—a glass of wine, a meal, and sleep. We spent the next day on several hiking trails leading to and along the coastline. The place had the charm and remote feeling of Kauai with its empty coves, but also the elegance and picturesque scenery of the San Francisco coast with deep blue waves crashing powerfully against boulders in the sea. We stared off into the distance; the horizon was marked only by the ocean, and there was no other land mass in sight. The air provided refreshing, clean relief. One could actually feel the natural energy of this place and I quickly realized why Aki wanted to come here.

That night, I marinated steak and barbecued for her neighbors: two surfer boys in their early thirties, their wives, and three kids. It made sense that they lived in Shimoda, a remote surfer town with no hassles. The mentality was starkly different from that of the overworked, overstressed city dwellers. We had a rather extravagant feast consisting of shrimp, steak, chicken, sausage, potatoes, salad, and paella for six of us.

After some glasses of champagne, I relayed stories of my college days and my Chinese roommate, along with my pot-smoking adventures. Both guys were intrigued as I elaborated on how much I smoked in college. Aki listened in disbelief, as if she had met me for the first time.

After dinner, the two women nonchalantly helped clean all the dishes. Their genuine care and respect for their elder, Aki, was obvious, signifying a remarkable cultural strength. There was no ego involved. It was then that I vowed to marry a nice Japanese woman.

Our guests left after dinner and as I finished cleaning the table, I noticed that one of the young men had forgotten his jacket. I grabbed it and rushed outside, down the stairs, and over to his house. They were already in their home. I rang the doorbell and one of the two guys hesitantly opened the door. He looked at me and breathed a sigh of relief.

"Come in!" he urged.

"Well, I actually just wanted to give you your jacket back."

"Oh, thank you. Come sit down."

He pulled the door open completely to a sight that surprised me: the whole group was sitting around a pipe, smoking weed as the kids played with their toys. It all connected at that point and I realized why they were so fascinated with my stories about smoking marijuana. They were complete stoners themselves.

"Take some!" the wife said, approaching me with the pipe.

They had done a complete 180 from a few minutes before. It was like an underground culture had forced them to be proper and polite outside, but inside their homes, free from the scrutinizing judgmental traditional culture, they were pot-smoking surfers.

"Hey, don't tell Aki we smoke," warned the guy who had opened the door.

It was funny and unexpected. Best of all, the woman I had just seen cleaning the dishes so politely and respectfully was now giggling and taking rips from the pipe as well. Stoned out of my mind a good twenty minutes later, I headed back to Aki's house, thinking that she might be getting worried. I also didn't want her to come looking for me.

"What took so long?" she asked.

The paranoia of the marijuana sunk into my mind.

"Oh, nothing—just hanging out. Talking."

"I was getting worried."

"Well, um . . . I'm back now."

She looked at me and I assumed the worst. She could smell the marijuana and see my bloodshot eyes. I didn't want to wait as she continued to examine me, or so I thought.

"I'm really tired, I'm going to go to sleep."

Somewhat uncharacteristically, I headed up the stairs and forced myself to sleep.

~

The first few days of the new year were quiet as I anticipated John's visit from the U.S. He had reserved a room in Tokyo's Peninsula Hotel, one of the top luxury hotels in Tokyo. Looking like an out-of-place vagabond, I lugged my heavy backpack and Aikido gear onto the train, through the packed stations, and into the lobby of the five-star hotel. In the sharpest contrast, John had arrived at the hotel in its chauffeured Rolls Royce. He never missed the opportunity to travel in first-class style.

The first sight of John was unexpectedly emotional. I had somehow forgotten the life I had and the comforts that surrounded me there. I had become so used to the life of a nomad that I had begun to think it was a permanent reality. Nevertheless, I was a pushover for these luxurious amenities and I wasted no time in enjoying them.

However, I was soon reminded of the stress and fast-paced culture with which I was all too familiar. John reminded me just how it had been in San Francisco—the need to be everywhere at once; the need to constantly be doing something as if on autopilot. It was evident in his slightly nervous undertone, his mental preoccupation, and every word and nonverbal gesture that John communicated. Still, I looked past it and enjoyed this chance to be with a great friend. For the first extended length of time during my more than six months of travel, I was able to let my guard down with a friend that I had known for ten years.

"Let's pop a bottle of champagne," John offered, as we walked across the room.

On the table by the expansive windows overlooking the Royal Palace, some thirty floors up, was a bottle of Dom Perignon sitting on ice.

"This is definitely one way to do it."

"You deserve it, bro. You've been living a tough life and I admire you for it. I want to know everything that's happened so far."

It was nice to pop a couple bottles of Dom Perignon, to reserve a table at a five-star restaurant and order Kobe beef from the top floor of the hotel, staring out onto the city lights as I caught up with my best friend.

After dinner, we took the hotel's Rolls Royce service for a night on the town and our luxury chauffeured transport caught the eyes of curious onlookers who were hoping to glimpse celebrities. I had quickly changed lifestyles, going from rags to riches in a couple of hours.

The next morning, I woke up with my first hangover in a while, quickly reminding myself of how bad it felt.

"Dude, I feel like shit," I told John, looking for some comfort.

"Tell me about it."

"Haven't drank that much in a while. Haven't felt like this in a while. I might puke. Worst of all, there was nothing going on."

"Don't worry man, I got something perfect for you right now."

John had arranged for a morning massage.

As much as that massage relaxed me, our rush to pack took it out of me as we grabbed our stuff—surprised at how much we had actually unpacked in less than a night—and ran for the *shinkansen* (bullet train) as fast as we could. We made it to our seats with two minutes to spare.

"How fast do think this bullet train is actually going?" I asked John as we zoomed through the different cities.

"Sixty miles per hour," he guessed with indifference.

"Are you kidding me? It's going at least 200 miles per hour."

"No way! Wanna bet? Winner gets a beer."

"I'm so hungover. I hope I lose," I said.

Luckily, there was an app for that. John's iPhone had a speedometer app that could gauge the traveling speed. We eagerly watched as the speed started increasing until it settled at 150 miles per hour. I won and reluctantly sipped the beer.

We took the bullet train to the commercial city of Nagano. From there, we hopped on a bus that transferred us all the way into the small town of Hakuba, where the only light the town received was from Christmas tree lights and sparsely distributed pole lights. A minivan from our hotel picked us up and out popped a short middle-aged Japanese man in a suit and rain boots.

"Hello, Hotel La Neige?" he asked hesitantly, half hiding behind the hood of the car.

"Yes."

With that confirmation, he jumped out from behind the hood confidently and quickly grabbed our bags as the snow poured heavily on our heads. He bounced around as he put our luggage in the trunk of the minivan, greeting us with pure unwavering excitement. I had never seen someone so excited to see people he had never met. Being the traditional conservative guys we were, John and I checked in and headed straight towards the wine bar, whose sign we had seen on the drive to the hotel.

As we walked in, an even more eccentric yet observant version of Johnny Depp, with long curly blond hair and piercing green eyes, was standing behind the bar. The dark wooden cabin construction was only made darker by the dimly lit track lights. The establishment was no more than six bar stools behind a wooden counter. On the bar sat a round ball of aged meat and behind the bar, wine glasses of different shapes and sizes. The bartender examined us closely and got us a couple of beers.

"Where you guys in from?"

"America," John responded without a thought.

"What part?"

"San Francisco."

"So you two homos are here together?" With that, remark, I looked up and noticed him smiling.

"Yeah, that's it." The ice was broken and a new friendship was born.

We started the night with his first suggestion, a Racer 5 straight out of Sonoma, California. I had come all the way to Japan only to learn about beers from my own backyard. We continued on to his more emphatic suggestion with the Double Daddy, and before I knew it I lost track of what I was drinking, now feeling the strong effect of the beer buzz. John and I left when we couldn't take anymore. Stumbling on the slippery snow-covered streets, John slipped onto his back as the snow poured down on us.

"Help me up, bro," John looked at me, eyes wide open, genuinely scared.

His eyes said it all. In that moment, he realized his vulnerability in this foreign country where he knew no one and was far from help. How quickly he had gone from a comfortable position to one where he was at the mercy of the circumstances. I was the only person who could help him. It was then, in this drunken state, that for a split second, John glimpsed the feeling of vulnerability I had experienced without a break over the last several months. In his eyes, I saw a deep understanding of my experience as a lone traveler through remote parts of Asia. I laughed it off, reminding him that this was nothing worthy of concern.

"Don't worry, bro, I got you."

"You're my best friend . . . Always there for me . . . I love you."

"Do me a favor."

"What?"

"Don't ever wear those cashmere shoes in the snow again."

"They're waterproof."

"Obviously, they're not drunk-proof."

We hit the sack and woke up at 11:00 AM the next day, too late to enjoy any of the fresh powder that had fallen the previous night.

The next night, we were back in the same wine bar to visit our new friend, Cal, the bartender.

"You guys rip up the powder today?" Cal asked.

"No, we were too hungover." Cal laughed with an obvious hint of contempt for our ineptitude.

"Well, I'm going out again tomorrow. Backcountry. You guys want to join? Locals only spot, best untouched pow."

"Sure, why not?"

"Be here at 7:30 AM on the dot. It's gonna be steep and deep," he said with a look that made us regret accepting his offer. He was going to kill us.

"Some of the grades will be thirty to thirty-five degrees. Be ready," he added.

We woke up and showed up five minutes late.

"What the fuck, you guys! I said fucking 7:30 AM. I'm fucking late!" Cal yelled.

We were so scared we were about to pee in our pants as we hopped into his dark brown Toyota minivan, which must have been a preserved piece from the '70s. Cal raced through the slippery streets as John and I held on to our seats, fearing for our lives. I doubted whether we would make it to the slopes alive.

*If he's this crazy in his driving, who knows what he'll put us through on the slopes?*

Cal pulled up to another hotel along the way and raced to the doors before coming out with two other kids about my age. Once everyone was in the vehicle, Cal was more eager than a child at a candy store, as if this were his first time.

"Here is your beacon in case you get stuck in an avalanche and here is a shovel in case you have to dig one of us out," Cal said as he handed us the implements.

I looked to John for an actual explanation of how to use these tools.

"Just hope you don't have to use them," he told me, leaving me completely helpless.

*Great, you really topped yourself this time, Dar. You didn't die in the deserts of Mongolia but today you will die backcountry skiing in Japan.*

We took a chairlift to the peak of the mountain and within a hundred feet of the chairlift dropoff, Cal ducked under red ropes clearly marking the boundaries of the mountain and disappeared into the steepest slope I had ever faced. I pulled up to the ropes and looked down. I couldn't see the slope below my snowboard, only a ledge as my board hung over the edge. I had to take a leap of faith and hope for the best as I watched John jump over the edge.

"Come on, you fuckers! Just go," Cal screamed from below.

The whole group jumped over the edge into a densely packed forest. We avoided trees with every turn, and I realized that John and I were the only idiots without helmets, skiing in the forest. As I slowly inched past each tree, Cal shredded the snow, slaloming through the trees as if by heart.

*How will they dig me out of an avalanche when they are fifty feet below me?*

And, as fate would have it, I triggered a small avalanche, watching the snow beneath my board give in and crumble down and me with it. I stayed on top as the trees gave me something to grasp. A potentially deadly situation avoided, I ducked under trees, steered around them, and caught up to the group.

"There's a ten-foot jump here! Hit that shit!" Cal yelled. There were trees within fifteen feet of the landing in every direction. There was no way I was going for it.

"No, Cal! I think I'm good." I said as I looked over to John on my right, who returned the glance with equal hesitation.

"Just hit the fucking jump, you pussy!" Cal continued screaming.

I came along the side of it, much to Cal's disappointment. A few seconds later I heard, "There's a manhole here over this jump; stay to the left!"

I turned to the left, trying to stay out of the manhole, but it was much larger than I anticipated. I jumped into the air, hoping to hop over it, but just didn't have enough speed, or air. I landed straight into it. With my lower body hanging in the hole and my upper body holding on for dear life on the surface, I mustered all the energy I had to extricate myself from the hole. It was "an every man for himself" attitude in the backcountry—I looked up to find no one in sight. I headed the only way to go: down. I was falling all over the place and getting more exhausted with every tumble because it took more effort to get up than it did to fall down or actually board. My legs burned, like they were in an oven, from the intense pressure I placed upon them. My mind was almost ready to give up. I stuck with it until I finally saw the group and the main trail just over the ridge.

"Let's hit that again but this time, start further back," Cal said with authority, like a true junkie.

That's when I realized just how crazy Cal was.

"No, I think I'll sit this one out," I told him, not wanting to experience that again.

John and I agreed to wait.

By the end of the day, we had done that same backcountry trail three times and I was completely exhausted in every part of my body. Needless to say, we spent the night at Cal's wine bar, drinking to temporarily mask our exhaustion and recounting our individual versions of the excursion.

∾

Just as abruptly as he had dropped into Japan, John was gone. I woke up hungover to a room full of High Chew candy wrappers. It was 11:00 AM and not only was I dehydrated, but I was also depressed to find myself alone again.

It is more difficult letting go of people when one knows that the journey ahead will be lonely. Lucky for me, Cal offered to pick me up and help me move to another lodge he had found. I ordered myself a final steak meal via room service and packed up my stuff, now heavier because of the snow gear John had brought from home.

The lodge, at an altitude of 6,000 feet, was nothing more than a bed and a nightly room charge of one hundred dollars. In the corner of the white-walled dungeon stood a small refrigerator. I went to it, hoping that given the nightly charge, the fridge would be fully stocked, but I was disappointed to find it completely empty. There was no TV, and, in fact, the only decent amenities were the new sheets and towels. I knew I had to get out but didn't know where else to go.

I had managed to secure a date with Hana, the cute bartender working at Cal's wine bar the previous night. Hana was an attractive half-Aussie, half-Japanese woman, here from Australia to work for her summer break.

Arriving at the wine bar a bit early, I sat at the bar. Cal immediately introduced me to a Japanese man who was owner of the Mominoki hotel next to the bar. The Mominoki hotel was one of the nicer ones, and after sweet-talking the owner, I got him to generously offer me a room with breakfast and dinner and access to the *onsen* (spa) for less than the price of a night at the lodge. Without any hesitation, I accepted his offer.

Hana and I had a boring and low-key date at a local, cozy restaurant she picked out; we were both slightly apprehensive about the other. I could barely drink the wine we ordered as I was still a little sick from the previous night's imbibing. I tried wrapping up the dinner quickly and heading back to the wine bar, my stomping ground. After seeing me with Hana, Cal took me aside.

"What are you doing with this girl?" he questioned sharply.

"Um, well, she's gorgeous."

"I know but it's a waste of your time. She's got a boyfriend back home and one out here. You take her to dinner?"

"Yes," I responded with regret creeping into my voice.

"Well, she's just going to take advantage of you, your money, and your kindness. I know her; she works for me."

"Well then, you better introduce me to some better girls. I'm starving here."

Little did I know what he had in store for me.

The following night there was to be a huge fire festival, bringing scores of young people into Hakuba to take the bus to the fire festival three hours away. I headed for the bus after a nap. Being alone, I was hoping to sit with someone I knew—perhaps Hana. However, while we waited to get on the bus, I spotted her with her sister and two guys. It didn't take me long to figure out that one of the men was her "guy" in Japan and that there wasn't room for a third suitor. She did manage a fleeting "hello" as she saw me standing in line to climb onboard. I was stuck with another solo traveler, a younger and slightly clueless Australian boy who had narrowly escaped being fired by Cal on numerous occasions.

Three hours later we arrived at Nozawa and it was literally "puking" snow, as the locals would describe. Three inches of fresh powder covered the ground, making it slippery for everyone. Like caged animals being let loose, we scattered in different directions. I was alone with no money and no ATM in sight to withdraw money to eat so I headed for the free sake. I saw two older Japanese men who were carrying a bundle of kindling that had been lit. Periodically, they would turn back and swing it randomly at people behind them, sometimes falling on their asses and laughing. Belligerent drunks, they were the best guides to lead me to the festival. In fact, they *were* the festival.

The festival was an odd rite of passage for young adults. The ages of twenty-five and forty-two are considered the most vulnerably unlucky ages; at the fire festival, in an effort to rid themselves of the evil, the forty-two-year-old participants would try to burn a tree. The twenty-five-year-olds were supposed to use their bodies to defend the tree from being scorched. The sight was bizarre. Dangerously drunk twenty-five-year-old men were swinging from ropes and dangling from the tree. I ducked under the ropes and joined them nonchalantly, but I stuck out like a sore thumb. Even the drunk twenty-five-year-old participants realized I didn't belong there.

As the event unfolded, a whole team of security held out ropes to separate the spectators from those actually involved in the festival. To make matters worse, it was snowing so hard I couldn't see and my jeans were soaked. A huge bonfire erupted and the older men gathered around it, lighting their huge batons and marching toward the young defenders. Their walk turned into a run. It was like a battle scene in *Gladiator*. They charged at these drunkenly dazed young danglers and slapped them with their fire batons. Round after round, the young men dropped right in front of me with their clothes burning. They were dragged off by a separate group.

After two hours of this surprisingly barbaric display, I moved out of the line of fire, literally, in search of shelter.

I stood in a souvenir shop for an hour until the buses were ready to leave again. The bus ride on the way back was a disaster. Hana and her boyfriend had fallen into the river and were shivering, uselessly trying to regain a sense of warmth. Hana's sister and her boyfriend were puking into a plastic bag, and the young woman sitting across the aisle from me was still drinking after six hours and counting. I passed out on the bus and once we arrived, I passed out instantly.

∼

The next night I returned to the wine bar to share my reactions to the festival with Cal. Midway through the night, Akemi, a twenty-seven-year-old woman John and I met a week before, arrived at the bar. A full-figured Japanese woman whose fashion sense was more outrageous than Madonna's in her younger days, Akemi emphasized her seductive nature with fishnet stockings, a short black skirt, and a blouse that advertised unashamedly her ample cleavage. A yoga enthusiast, she had the perfect body for it. Because she was speaking so eagerly to John the first night we met, I didn't get to talk to her at all. However, before long, she warmed up to me.

"What are you doing in Hakuba?"

"I'm actually just traveling through Japan. I spent two months at an Aikido *dojo*."

"Aikido?" she said, her interest piqued.

"Yeah, I was living in the *dojo* and practicing every day in the Mecca of Aikido."

"Wow," she said with admiration.

"After this I'm going to India to practice yoga in an ashram."

"I do bikram yoga here. It is the best thing you can do for your health."

"Yeah, you might have to show me a couple moves," I told her, smiling. "You want another beer?"

"Yes, I'd love one."

We both knew where we were going.

We drank a couple more beers and Cal took me aside by the bathroom.

"This is the girl you want to talk to," he told me, with a wink.

I returned to my seat at the counter, suggesting we go to the bar next door and dance to techno. Occasionally, she would run off to her friends, point me out and giggle, making me feel like a mannequin on display.

"What should we do now?" she asked at the end of the night, obviously waiting for my move.

"We both know exactly what we should do," I told her confidently.

"Yeah, what is that?"

"Let's go back to my room at the Mominoki and I'll tell you."

She giggled and put her arm in mine as we stumbled through the snow, across the street. The rest is history.

~

# PART FOUR

*India: Challenges of Enlightenment*

~

The first flight leg to Beijing was a piece of cake, just four hours. On the next leg of my journey, there was no mistaking my final destination. I was surrounded by Indians wearing turbans, robes, and saris. They were among the most aggressive passengers I have ever seen on a plane. The woman behind me pushed my seat completely forward with all her might to prevent me from reclining my seat. Meanwhile, the woman next to me woke me up twice to show her immigration card and say something in Hindi. I tried unsuccessfully to tell her that I didn't speak Hindi because she did the same thing a few minutes later. The seven-and-a-half-hour flight seemed like the *Seinfeld* episode where Elaine is exiled to the crammed economy section while Jerry and a drop-dead gorgeous blonde sip champagne in the ridiculously roomy first-class section. Arriving in Delhi, it was another hour before bags arrived and, even then, a bag would pop out every few minutes or so. Ready to scream a blue streak of expletives, I walked to the end of the conveyor and my luggage was there on the floor.

At the domestic terminal, I managed to find a row of seats and fell asleep. I waited three hours for a flight that likely would be delayed because of heavy fog. We boarded and my eyes brightened at the TVs embedded in the headrests. I watched an entire movie and an episode of *Two and a Half Men* before we departed. Then, we were instructed to deplane. Apparently, our plane wasn't going to Trivandrum (my destination) and our departure, already delayed by more than six hours, was set back even further. The passengers made such a fuss about our predicament that the airline promised to get us to our destination via another plane to another city followed by a taxi to Trivandrum. We returned to the airport and this time I found my sanctum in the Amex club lounge. Taking my father's identity, I convinced them that I had lost my card and once inside, I ordered the lounge employee to bring me food from a restaurant I saw in the terminal. She took my order and left to get it. I satisfied my ravenous appetite, eating an oddly exotic buffet of Western and Eastern treats—chocolate milkshake, a hummus platter, and Tandoori wraps. The crowning touch of my success was a brownie with ice cream.

My luck continued when we finally boarded the plane. My neighbor, Alyssa, turned out to be a young American woman working for the U.S. embassy in Delhi. The flight flew by. We landed in Kochi, a city five hours away from Trivandrum via taxi. Alyssa, a British couple, and I crammed into a taxi. The British woman blathered on and on about her experiences in India, which hardly qualified as great adventures.

It was already late Tuesday evening when we came across an elephant festival with two giant pachyderms bedecked in strands of jewels and people riding atop.

We stopped at my hotel and I didn't get a chance at a proper good-bye with Alyssa, as the British woman continued her inconsequential stories. As I grabbed my bag from the taxi driver, Alyssa jumped out of the car.

"Wait!"

I turned around to face her.

"Take this. Call me," she said, handing me a scrap of paper with her number scrawled on it.

The gesture brightened my otherwise disappointed look when I saw this modern hotel sitting amidst a community of ramshackle buildings and half-built mud huts. The streets were crudely paved but packed with stands and convenience stores offering everything from the Indian version of typical convenience store products to cheap clothes, street food, and fruits and vegetables.

The gritty scene only amplified my desire to go to the ashram deep in the jungle. Arriving at the gates of Neyar Dam the next day, the location evoked reverberating waves of rejuvenating energy—just what one would expect at the entrance of a dreamy paradise where the prize of connecting directly to one's soul was possible. The palm trees appeared surreal, unlike the romanticized artificial objects one might find in a jungle-themed restaurant or bar. The jungle's cacophony was a symphony of random animal noises, and the sight of birds, lizards, and spiders completed the picture. The lake tempted me with its beautiful turquoise veneer. Despite warnings that the lake was infested with alligators, people did not hesitate to jump into the waters; they were confident that the eight-year streak of no alligator attacks would continue. Never had I been in a place where the energy emanated so strongly.

I arrived just in time for dinner. It was customary to take off our sandals before heading into the dining room, where straw mats were laid out and a metal plate awaited each person. Volunteers served food out of a bucket and as they passed by, the image of a war camp prisoner emerged in my mind. What they served seemed to carry no more vitamins than a glass of water. My plate was filled with a weak, watery broth of tomatoes and potatoes. To add insult to injury, we had to wait until the whole ashram was seated, all the while listening to an Indian girl with a horrific voice chant to us.

The diet was strictly Ayurvedic, which is the ancient medical system of India. The food is vegan and prepared with no oil or salt. According to the Ayurvedic philosophy, each person is categorized as embodying too much of one of three constitutions, according to body and personality type. Our body comprises all three constitutions but too much of one in particular can cause problems such as laziness or too much energy, so it is important to eat in a way that reconciles any imbalances and ensures the proportions are appropriately harmonized for each individual.

Later that night, more than 200 people sat in a dark hall as we meditated and chanted. I sat uncomfortably on my new yoga mat and tried to cross my legs. This caused a whole new set of discomforts and aches in my knees and feet, sensations completely different from what I had experienced in the Japanese *dojo*.

"Watch your breath. Feel the silence. Visualize an object. Chant a mantra." The *swamiji* was mashing different types of meditation into one ridiculously complicated remix. I couldn't do all these at the same time.

I retired to my room, consisting of no more than a plank with a thin mattress lying atop it. Actually it was more like a cushion than a mattress; it was surrounded by a mosquito net that restricted me to the space within it. Two sheets were provided, one to put over the cushion and one to cover us. The climate was so scorching, though, that I doubted I would ever need the second cover. The room was like a college dorm, only with fewer amenities, dirtier floors, and no windows. Instead of windows, colorful drapes hung down the opening. I entered my mosquito net coffin and comfortably fell asleep.

The next day—a Thursday—should have been the beginning of my education, but it actually was the last day of a two-week yoga vacation seminar. While all the vacationers were easily performing the headstand, I could barely manage to sit cross-legged. To make matters worse, the young beautiful Italian woman next to me was wearing see-through black spandex. The naturally erotic sideshow became an insurmountable distraction, but it managed to mitigate the long uncomfortable yoga session. Breakfast also proved to be a major disappointment. We had the same meal as dinner the night before: steamed vegetables and rice.

At least the news that there were other Iranians in the ashram temporarily made me forget the disgusting food. There were ten Iranian women whose ages ranged from twenty-three to fifty-two and Dariush, a younger man whose age was never revealed. I quickly opened up the line of communication at the snack shack by asking Dariush about his home roots in Farsi. From there, we spent the rest of the day speaking in Farsi. As we munched on jagged almond snack balls, I recounted my experience of the first class.

"There was this girl right next to me with her . . . I think they were Italian . . . and her pants were literally see-through. I could see her red thong in every exercise. In fact you should have seen the downward dog. How am I supposed to do the fish pose in these circumstances?"

Dariush looked on with a huge smile on his face.

"I mean, do you think she doesn't know? I'm sure she knows and wants everyone to look."

Dariush watched the edge of our table as I spoke. The Italian woman's friend sat alone. I paid her no attention but Dariush fixated his gaze on her.

"You know that girl you keep looking at is the Italian's friend," I told him.

"Yeah, you know she's Persian. Right?"

"What?"

"She's sitting there listening to every word you say," he whispered.

I looked back over as she stood with a satisfied smile on her face. Obviously, she knew precisely about whom we were chatting about and, after that, I never again saw the sexy Italian woman.

The ashram had plenty of people—300—so it was easy to make other friends. Marieke, my first female friend, was a tall German woman with a stunning figure introduced to me by Dariush. Before long, she and I became close friends, too. She had the calm temperament of a still pond. Nothing ever seemed to shock or faze her, even swimming in a lake filled with alligators.

We made plans to skip the boring lecture for a swim.

"You hear about the alligators in this lake?" she asked me.

"What?"

"Yeah, they say there are alligators, but no one has been attacked for eight years."

"Is that supposed to calm me down?"

"Yes," she said coyly.

An ashram employee overheard our voices.

"Excuse me, but you guys cannot be here. It is lecture time and you must go to the lecture hall."

We were caught. There was no way out, or so we thought. But I had a plan.

"Okay, sure." I said to the monitor before Marieke had a chance to say anything.

I grabbed her hand and walked her back to the lecture hall, glancing surreptitiously behind me at the monitor. The minute he looked away, we darted into the high jungle vegetation, completely out of his sight. We popped out in an area of the lake where no one could see us. The thrill of playing hooky was exhilarating. Our hearts were both beating fast; we were like mischievous kids, but old enough to be erotically romantic.

"Let's go for a swim," she suggested as she took off her shirt, revealing for the first time her toned stomach and upper legs.

"Okay," I told her, stripping off my shirt as well.

She jumped in, splashed, and went off into the distance.

*You can't be a baby, Dar, but is it worth getting your leg bit by an alligator?*

I decided to go for it and went out to the middle of the lake with her.

"Let's go to the other side," she suggested.

*Enough is enough. I've already humored her by going all the way to the middle of the lake. I am going no further.*

"No, that's enough for me."

I pretended to head back and dove underwater, coming up behind her. I clutched her leg firmly as she let out a scream that I was surprised the monitor didn't hear.

"Holy shit, you scared me," she yelled.

"I know. You got to watch out for the alligators out here. Now, you ready to go back?"

She agreed and we returned to a nice afternoon session of yoga facing the sunset as we relaxed in our *asanas*. I was on cloud nine—until I met Dayita, a Tibetan-Indian slender beauty whose beautiful black hair seemed too perfectly soft and straight to be natural—the kind of hair women want and spend hours a day straightening. Her aura emanated grace in every way she moved, as if she was floating from place to place.

We held each other's gaze the first time we saw each other from across the crowded courtyard at teatime. Her long black hair fell with a naturally artistic touch upon her shoulders. She looked at me for longer than one would glimpse at someone in passing, but the gaze did not seem like a stare. Rather, it was a realization of suspended time, a long moment when two eyes meet for the first time and two souls recognize each other.

We didn't actually speak until a couple days after that encounter. Fate obviously had a hand in timing here, so it was no coincidence that I ran into her as I was cutting *satsang*, the daily ritual when we meditated, chanted, and chatted with the guru.

"Skipping *satsang*?" she said with a smile that instinctively warmed my heart.

"Yeah, I'm just too tired."

"That's not good."

"I could be telling you the same thing," I said, rather defensively.

"I left for just a second, I was going back," she retorted.

"I'm sure it was just a second. And what were you doing out of *satsang* anyway?"

"It was!" she said, with a smile on her face confessing her mischievous act.

Indeed, it was not just a second. We both welcomed the diversion as we sat for hours outside in the humid air, recounting our journeys and experiences so far at the ashram.

"You know, I can see things sometimes," she said with a detectable if not slight tone of terror in her voice.

"Yeah, like souls?"

"Like ghosts that haunt me."

The air grew thick and silent.

"What do you see now?" I asked.

"Something right next to you. But I don't want to get into it."

This was my dream girl: as crazy if not crazier than me, and she didn't beat around the bush about it. We felt comfortable with each other in that first conversation, missing all of *satsang* in order to catch up on one another's spiritual lives and philosophies.

"I have always wanted to spend time in a monastery in Nepal," I told Dayita as she laughed in disbelief.

"What's so funny?" I said, with just a tinge of embarrassment.

"My family is the head of several monasteries around India. I think it not just a coincidence that I met you."

Her laugh wasn't mocking, but rather one of disbelief. She even believed that there were no coincidences. There was nothing left to doubt as we both knew our being in the ashram at the same time was intended to occur. But neither of us would completely admit it—at least not yet.

∾

I signed up for a ten-dollar Ayurvedic massage at the ashram, not knowing what that entailed. Luckily, I had opted out of the *pancha karma*, a twenty-one day complete body cleansing massage and diet that had you throwing up and using feces and oil to clean out your entire system. One simple massage would have to be enough.

I was led into a room with a wooden plank on center stage. That was to be my massage bed. The masseur pulled out a bottle of ghee, or clarified butter oil. I eased into the bed's stiffness as the warm buttery textures softened my skin as well as the plank my body rested on. The experience was intoxicating as the masseuse moved from my back and legs to my head. He shoved ghee into my ears and finally poured it on my forehead through a swinging funnel above my head, allowing it to dribble into my eyes. Despite the intense discomfort of not being able to smell, hear, or see, I held on to the belief that this would cleanse my body.

Blind and hurting, I was led to the shower where I desperately tried to get all the ghee out of every orifice of my body, but no matter how hard I tried it wouldn't come out of my eyes and ears. I left feeling like I was deteriorating. By the time I left the shower, I still had oily ears and felt more uncomfortable. By nightfall, I was vomiting and lying helplessly in bed. To make matters worse, a new roommate arrived. Not only was I sick and vulnerable, but I had to deal with the awkwardness of meeting a complete stranger, with whom I was supposed to share my personal space. Fortunately, Dariush was kind enough to watch out for me, delivering tea and food to my room between classes. It was odd because he never attended any class. He simply stayed in his room and practiced his calligraphy and *setar*, an ancient Persian instrument similar to a banjo or guitar.

"The classes here are not advanced enough for me," he explained. "The moves I do are more advanced than what they show in class," he boasted.

All those I spoke to in the ensuing days about the Ayurvedic massage explained that it makes one sick but only because the toxins are leaving the body. I doubted the veracity of this because it didn't make sense that I had to go through so much pain to detoxify myself. The feeling fortunately lasted no longer than a day and a half.

～

The ashram had a tradition of a silent walk to the lake where we would sit, chant, and observe the beauty of nature. Dayita and I were walking together, not as silently as we should have, when she told me about "the other guy." There was another guy at the ashram that she had fallen for before I arrived. I didn't understand the gravity of this revelation until I saw how truly reluctant she was to fall for me despite all things working against her. Never had I thought this was the scene for a rebound relationship.

"You don't understand. I really liked him. And think I still might," she said, her words cutting through me like a knife.

"He fooled me into thinking he was genuine."

He wasn't. He wanted what every guy wanted but veiled it under the guise of wanting to be a long-term volunteer at the ashram and eventually a monk. He had fooled her quite effectively, because while she took her time getting to know him, his impatience got the better of him, making him find another woman who was not nearly as hesitant. Dayita was heartbroken and betrayed.

Nevertheless, I was at the bottom of the heartbreak chain—being heartbroken by the woman who was heartbroken. My world tumbled severely. My happy-go-lucky world of love discovered in the most natural yet unexpected ways had been crushed by the harsh truth that smacked me back into a place of utter reality. I felt like Neo in *The Matrix* seeing the real world for the first time—dark, desolate, and dead.

She played a constant game with me, toying with my emotions either intentionally or unconsciously. I was a cat trying to claw at a dangling string always just out of my reach.

"Let's run away together," she said with spontaneous impulse one day, as we sat outside on the lawn between classes.

"Okay," I said without hesitation.

"No . . . we can't. I just can't do it."

I had fallen for the trick. She had me wrapped around her finger and we both knew it. My error in admitting I wanted to leave with her was, at that moment, fatal for the prospects of securing her emotions for me.

"I need to just get back to my home after this. I haven't seen my family in a long time and they need me," Dayita continued. "But you were the one I was supposed to meet . . . not him. He was just like you in every way—looks, personality, thoughts, but he tricked me. He was missing an essence. But I still don't know if I can be hurt again."

She was constantly yanking my chain and throwing jabs that made me fall for her again and again. With each stirring, when I thought it was for real, she would tamp me down, reminding me that she could not just give into her heart so rashly.

As my romance with Dayita wobbled shakily and continuously between hope and despair, my effective capacity to plumb deeper into my *asanas* was inversely related. I went off into another realm of depth and solitude that was painful to get out of once yoga was over. My emotions, meditations, and yoga were draining me physically and emotionally. I was losing control of myself.

## ⌒ 20 ⌒

The following night, after our consistent nightly talks, I made the fatal error of revealing all of my cards verbally to Dayita. Something about the ashram brought only honesty from me. I was unable to hold anything back, as if I had been injected with a truth serum. I had no control over myself, nor was I able to play my cards close to my chest. My crush betrayed more sensible instincts, especially given that she was bearing scars from past relationships. Admittedly, I was bewitched in a trance of intense love. She obviously did not admit to feeling the same way, but my instincts told me she did. I found it an unfortunate twist of irony that she prided herself on the thrill of the adventure but nevertheless shied away from taking full advantage of the opportunity.

Unfortunately, the mind leaves little real room for spontaneity. Willing to follow my most vulnerable risks, I felt drunk with love and wanted to be the one to help her conquer her fears of disappointing personal and intimate relationships. But, then again, there are the hopelessly unchangeable hard wiring differences between men and women. Obviously, Dayita was thinking long term and logically. She was conserving herself from another disappointment mentally and physically, especially as we were from different countries and were eventually going to part ways in the coming weeks. Whatever her reason, she

maintained her guard despite facing the plainest demonstration of deep love.

At breakfast, I noticed that my appetite had
improved. I ate more than twice my normal amount and
actually enjoyed it. My *chakras* had been opened up and I
was reborn. Meanwhile, Dayita was getting ready to leave
the ashram for a few days to see a friend leave.

"Do you want me to come back?" she asked me.

"Yes, I do," I told her as honestly as I always managed.

"Okay, then after my friend leaves, I will return."

"When?"

"I'll be back before the Siva festival."

The Siva festival was to be an entire day of nonstop
chanting and praising of Lord Siva. By dinner on festival
day, I still hadn't seen Dayita and was beginning to think
that she might not return as promised. After dinner, I followed the entire ashram group to the outdoor area where
we were expected to chant all night. Once the ceremony
started, the *swami* instructed us to line up and pour ghee
into the fire and make an offering of a certain herb to
Siva. I stood next to a beautiful young woman whose
tresses hung low past her torso and whose skin was an
olive tone that one might see on a magazine cover. She
glowed in every respect and her smile was all that was
needed to trigger an all-night conversation. She was Ivy,
a Palestinian woman my age from Los Angeles and had
been traveling India for the last three months. She had
completed the teacher's training course and was getting
ready to move on the next day.

It was a relief to speak the American form of English
without having to explain slang or idioms. It had been
a long time since I could use "like" or "hella" or "sick,"
and I felt closer to her because of this bond of cultural

communication. I would never have expected to be standing at an all-night chanting ceremony in remote India next to someone with whom I could speak so easily; I didn't not worry about anything in the world. The Siva ceremony was magical in its effect.

I did not expect Dayita to show up during the ceremony, but she did, and she glared at me with obvious jealousy. There wasn't much I could do at this point so I continued talking to Ivy until she excused herself to retrieve her drum. I made my first contact with Dayita and we said hello. I returned to my spot in the squared-off garden as the dancing began. Several lady friends joined me in the dance and before long Ivy entered the group. Dayita watched from a distance as she chatted with another fellow. The tables had turned and I no longer felt chained to her. I was set free on this night. She didn't join the dance, but she did sit right across from my spot, trying to be as discreet as possible in tracking every movement of mine.

After what felt like three hours, Ivy and I checked the time to find out that only an hour had gone by. We continued dancing and talking until midnight.

"I really wish I could charge my iPod before I leave tomorrow," Ivy said.

"Well, I have a charger if you want to use it."

Her eyes lit up with excitement. She went to get her iPod so that I could charge it for her and followed me to my room. The air was so light and relaxed and I enjoyed the contrast of being as light and carefree as one could possibly be after being weighed down for so long. At the moment, Ivy's light-hearted mood was much more appealing than the deep, profoundly philosophical sobering tone of Dayita.

I told Ivy about my obsession with picking continuously at my hair and she was amused by my admission of this small tic. She clearly was trying to discern my deeper thought processes but not using the same piercing approach Dayita usually applied. I began going through my traveling pictures while playing Julio Iglesias for her, admitting freely how much I loved him for his singing. That apparently was enough foreplay for her, as we started kissing. Ivy's body was a gift of incredible flexibility, thanks to her extensive experience in yoga and naturally limber body. Mine wasn't bad either. Perhaps this is what people mean when they talk about the phenomenal benefits of Tantric lovemaking. The night was comfortable, casual, and carefree, the perfect antidote for what I had been feeling until that day.

The next morning, Ivy asked if I would join her in Varkala, a popular beach town for kids to hang out at on their days off, and I agreed to go along, meeting her at a restaurant at noon. At least I was able to recharge my body after our night of excellent sex. I decided that I would talk to Dayita before I left. I missed my opportunity, as she was already gone.

"Daria!" I turned around. Andrea, a cute young German woman, caught up with me.

"I'm going to Goa next week. Do you want to come with me?"

The epitome of a hippie, Andrea was cool and calm with her blue eyes, blonde dreads, cotton off-white pants, and faded blue shirt. I decided that anything to get out of the ashram was a good idea.

"Sure, I'll join you."

That night, I packed, all the while worried that I had yet to receive a fully confirmed travel itinerary. All I had was a receipt indicating the itinerary would arrive within twenty-four hours. The problem was that my flight was scheduled to depart within a shorter timeframe. And I had not yet booked any accommodations in Goa.

"Dayita, I'm leaving tomorrow," I said, realizing that our relationship was coming to an unfulfilled culmination.

"Okay, I'm going to come say goodbye in a little while. Wait for me. I need to speak to Ananda," she told me, trying to mask her sadness. Ananda was an Indian guy in the ashram who had also fallen for Dayita. Obviously, I was not her only victim. She walked out of my room and returned a minute later.

"Aren't you going to ask for my email address? Aren't we going to keep in touch?"

Though I expected her to return, I was a bit taken aback that she gave in so quickly. She gave me her email and left without another word.

After about an hour, she showed up again and started to read *The Tibetan Book on Living and Dying* in my bed, hardly a confident signal for me to pursue any ideas of foreplay. I just couldn't believe she didn't feel comfortable enough to talk directly with me. So I took it to the next level and started singing Julio Iglesias to her—the same foreplay which had inspired and motivated Ivy previously. I continued, kissing her body and undressing her, but she abruptly intervened and turned the tables on this dance of foreplay. The domination play had been the one strategy I had not yet used. I always knew that she feared giving into me, but enough was enough and it was time for me to take charge of the situation. Deep down, I knew she wanted me to do so, as if this was a test of my manhood.

This time, she looked at me vulnerably as I removed her pants and then her underwear. She was committed and we both knew there was no going back. As we made love, I noticed her eyes, wide open in bliss and in agony. She had given in to me completely. However, I realized that this was not my victory of superiority or dominance. Rather, it was a mutual acknowledgment of good faith and trust. It was her final admission that I would be an acceptable steward, sensitive to her vulnerabilities. In return, I had the understanding that I would respect rather than abuse and take exploitative advantage. As I rolled over her, she looked at me in complete submission. Dayita's innocence at the moment seemed so fragile, as if I held in my hands the world's thinnest glass and the tiniest bit of pressure would break it. Our emotional energies were as deeply rooted as a century-old redwood tree. Her eyes at times burst open in a strange yet exhilaratingly painful delight as I was her and she was me and there was no longer any separation between us. The warmth, the emotions, the passion, the vulnerability, and the primal instincts blended together into the most beautiful act of love I had ever experienced.

Afterward, we lay next to each other, speaking as if we had just met for the first time and, in a way, we had. We had never known this side of one another, with both our guards completely relaxed. There was nothing more to be gained. We had completely given into each other. She revealed her true self to me. This genuineness was what I had anticipated from the moment I saw her at the ashram, the side I was waiting to be let in on. It was ranked as my most unforgettable night.

∽

The next day, another chapter in this journey was closed. I believed that with each stop, I was becoming better at remaining detached and avoiding strong emotional attachments. I was definitely getting used to seeing the stream of people entering and leaving the ashram, much as I witnessed at the *dojo* back in Japan. I took a good deal of pride in becoming a veteran at mastering the discipline to take the lessons from each stop—whether it was the ger, *dojo*, a Balinese beach surf school, or the ashram—and inculcating them in my daily life. Leaving Dayita at this point was not difficult, because somehow I sensed that she would not let me go so easily after all the time we had invested in our relationship. I told her I was going to Goa and she was welcome to visit. It would be the perfect tonic for any tensions that may have been simmering inside.

After a final kiss from Dayita, I hopped in the taxi and headed to the airport, hoping that an unlucky string of flight delays would be finally broken. However, the reservations agent bore the inevitable news and added that I might miss my connecting flight to Goa and would have to sleep in Mumbai for the night.

In India, time does not seem to be a highly valued commodity.

In Goa, away from the less-than-palatable Ayurvedic diet, I decided to drown the sorrows of my loneliness at a restaurant buffet. A vegetable curry with an ominously red tint was extremely spicy—certainly the spiciest thing I had eaten in a few months. This jolted my system almost immediately as my body had become so habituated to the salt-less, oil-less bland Ayurvedic regimen. Ten minutes later, I stared at a hole in the ground and a water hose next to it, regretting having ever touched the curry. Who knew vegetable curry could be so dangerous? The proprietors of the restaurant weren't kind enough to even leave toilet paper for a sorry foreigner like me.

I was in a holding pattern the next day, waiting for Andrea or Dayita to arrive, and the ramshackle hut didn't help. Here in lowly Palolem, the surroundings would have sapped even the most energetic and optimistic individual. The eyesore of the makeshift straw huts on the beach held up by stilts weighed on my psyche. It was often too difficult to distinguish one from another when it came to finding a place to eat. Just painting these forlorn buildings in bright vibrant colors or adding intense, graphic murals would have dramatically changed the landscape and energized a tired visitor. My initial perceptions of Goa immediately discounted the "Chamber of Commerce" pitch one often sees in brochures or travelogues about Goa being the place of choice for foreigners coming to India. Expecting tranquility, serenity, and empty beaches was the objective, but it was dismaying to think that one would have to navigate a large center of poverty and junk to arrive at a destination that was not even all it was cracked up to be.

I was still trying to handle "outside" food, which continued to sicken me after every meal. After several weeks at the ashram, my body had been too cleansed to take on the thick curries, spices, and excess oil they served here. I ended up spending half my day in the bathroom.

Biding my time, I spent one night in my room meditating and doing yoga, which proved to be more satisfying personally because I could practice at my own pace and improvise a bit. I particularly enjoyed doing a variation of a handstand, which would not have been allowed at the ashram. On the matter of diet, I wanted to maintain the principles of the Ayurvedic diet with some leeway but, in Goa, it was damn near impossible to find a decent restaurant that resisted the impulse to do a culinary mashup of Indian, Mexican, Chinese, and Italian cuisines—often all in one entrée.

I also attempted to follow some semblance of discipline in my daily meditation regimen. According to Sivananda's book on meditation, one should awaken between 4:00 AM and 6:00 AM to start. I set my alarm for 4:00 AM but couldn't get up until 6:00 AM. I planned on meditating for thirty-five minutes and set my alarm for that. After what felt like twenty minutes, I couldn't take it anymore and decided to stop. When I looked at the clock, I was surprised to see that fifty minutes had actually passed. It was a triumph to have had surpassed my objective.

Of course, I had other challenges in store. I had to figure out my arrangements to go to the formidable and imposing Vipassana retreat, which I already knew would be my most rigorous encounter in this journey. I knew that I was getting closer to home base. Traveling until now was a great deal more difficult than I had imagined at the outset when I planned this transcontinental journey, and I feared the hardest part was yet to come. More insistently, I had to battle pangs of homesickness and weak moments of yearning to abort this trip. Nepal, my final destination, was on the horizon, and I anticipated that in about a month and a half I would be joining monks at a monastery where I could perfect my technique for meditation just as I had done with Aikido and yoga.

Whatever uncertainties I had about anything else, I was absolutely convinced that Dayita would come, just as she returned the night of the Siva festival. Needless to say, I knew she would make her decision at the last possible moment. I waited on the beach through the evening and then at about two in the morning, I returned to my room. Just as I was about to close the door, I saw her unmistakable form off in the distance. Though this place may have called itself a resort, it was no more than a collection of ten or so huts. I moved closer to be sure it was her. At that moment, she swung around and her eyes caught mine.

Our reunion was precarious and tentative. I guess both of us were trying to keep whatever strong passions we had for each other in check for at least a moment or so. But my stomach was doing jumping jacks and my heart's thumping was strong enough to burst out of my rib cage. I wanted to catch her up on everything I had done since the day we were separated.

"You know, I've been waking up every morning at six to meditate for an hour and I do yoga in the evenings."

"Really?!" she seemed simultaneously impressed and in disbelief.

That evening, I stuck to my word and we carried our mats to the beach. There was a deserted inlet I had seen which I knew would be ideal for yoga. As we watched the sunset, she stood over me, helping me in my *asanas*, going deeper into each pose in order to get it right. It was funny to think that a day before I was looking around for a class to join and now I had a certified teacher, and one to whom I was attracted. The locals couldn't take their eyes off my newfound teacher, envious of what I had discovered.

I shared with her my compilation of musings about life while she stared at me in disbelief. I had written about our societal collapse and people's inability to look past success and wealth in search of happiness. She could not believe that I was preaching the Buddhist doctrine word for word without knowing it. As we spoke, time was floating, meaningless. The world was on pause in order for us to catch up. The hours and eventually the days came and went without our noticing it.

Anxious to rid myself of the beaten-down vibe of Palolem, I booked a room for Dayita and me at the Hyatt Resort for two nights. Upon entering the gates of the Hyatt, I felt as if I was floating on bubbles. The service, the landscaping, even the energy seemed so much more upbeat. I was practically jumping off the walls as we entered our room: a bona fide shower with a shower head and a hand-held spout, a bath tub, great natural lighting, a clean toilet, air conditioning, a balcony, a mini bar. It was great to reconnect with these amenities. Like in Japan, I had forgotten the pleasures of luxury.

I ran to book a massage at the hotel spa, then headed to the beach to order drinks and eat a salad, deciding to be steadfast in following a vegetarian regimen. I was so excited that I didn't know where to start. At the bar, I

had my first taste of alcohol in four weeks, which provided a great deal of happiness. Dayita joined me and
I ordered her a Long Island. We drank and reminisced
about our experiences soaking ourselves at the ashram's
lake after a hot afternoon session.

I felt completely liberated from the ashram—free to
express unashamedly my love for Dayita in public and
to order food without concern for strict dietary consid-
erations. I ordered Tandoori chicken and pigged out,
not remembering until later how bloated one gets from
Indian meat dishes. Despite that, I still ordered three
scoops of ice cream, finally succeeding at having Dayita
try my favorite sweet indulgence.

$\backsim$ 22 $\backsim$

Everything seemed perfect in this break from the seri-ous emotional burdens associated with this journey. I'm still a sucker for modern luxurious amenities like the five-star resort, my safety zone, where every wish and desire is tended to and worry and stress are forbidden terms. There the most stress comes from deciding what to order among the abundant and tempting options on the menu. My only regret is not having enough time to taste everything. Even though I was "vegetarian" at the moment, tandoori chicken and chicken tikka masala were an exception to my diet.

I truly wish that everyone in the world could take a couple months off just to experience the highs of luxury and then return to their lives with a newfound energy. Lately home had been looking better and more vivid in my imagination. I pictured it: the smell of my dogs attentively sitting next to me, along with the warmth of my bed—the comfort of being home. I saw the beauty of our house in a different, more graceful, light. I could feel the rays of sun shining through the tall windows of our entryway and remember the intense feeling of joy I would experience walking into the house without notic-ing it. I couldn't see how truly happy I was. The anchor of home was sorely missed, as was the familiarity of life surrounding the home. However, amid that euphoric sense of nostalgia a sobering, grimmer reality bled into that bright image. The expense to experience this luxury was enormous, even before paying for the privilege. It seemed like a perpetually unfair return on investment: work over ten hours a day so one could experience an occasional—even rare—couple of hours of blissful pampering in a resort or vacation enclave—and that is if you were one of the fortunate ones. Even during a temporary period of blithe enjoyment, we're never really far away from the imposing demons of work and exhaustion. What choice do we have? In Goa, the answer was very much unclear. I guess this was the big question to be confronted on this journey.

Back home, downtown Tiburon, CA has its own brand of beauty and enchantment. There are picturesque bistros and cafes, and verdant walking paths along the waterway that provide soothing views of the urban skyscape. Drive three minutes from my home and I'm at the club to play tennis with a friend. Life is blissful. Add in conveniences of air conditioning, a toilet seat with a full commode, and an electric bidet, and the picture gets substantially fuller.

*But was I truly happier?*

As much as I appreciated these amenities, I also realized that the enjoyment of such amenities came at a cost.

The following day, all Dayita and I had was the name of a popular bar in a town. The destination was an hour away. We hopped in a taxi and headed out. Once we approached the bar's location, the driver grew impatient. He argued with us, insisting that he drop us off immediately. We drove up and down the thoroughfare, with people poking their heads in the taxi window, asking us if we were looking for a place to stay. However, along the way, I saw a place that looked as close to a Tuscan villa as one could possibly imagine in India. That was where we decided would be the best place to stop.

The place consisted of a set of one-story duplexes surrounding a pool and lawn. The rooms had a TV, a bed, and a shower—bare necessities in a contemporary world. Because it looked reasonable and the price was decent, we moved in, taking up shelter once again in a place we would call home for the next few days. We didn't spend much time out of the room other than to get ice cream. Laziness had taken over us like the plague and Dayita and I spent two days exchanging teachings on her orthodox strict understanding of Buddhism and my New Age gray-bordered understanding of the world around me. It was a clash of rigidity and looseness as we discussed our opinions.

"Why do you think that life must be so serious?" I asked.

"Life is a serious thing."

"Why can't it be enjoyed?"

"We have come here for far too important things to take it lightly."

"Well, wouldn't one of our goals here be to find happiness?"

The conversation continued in this manner, as Dayita tried to explain the seriousness of life while I countered with lack of order and discipline. It was a reflection of selves. Though we argued, we never became upset at one another. We were so in love that we always understood that the force of our relationship was greater than the unleashed tension of our arguments.

I stayed in contact with Esta, a Dutch DJ I had met at the ashram, who apparently was in another town called Vagator. She was going to DJ that night so Dayita and went to see her. The place consisted of small dirty tables with enough room to place a couple beers, bamboo chairs well past their prime, and dirty floors. I felt like I was at Skid Row in Cabo, Mexico. Its one redeeming quality was its beautiful view of the sunset. After a few drinks, Esta swung by to chat.

"How's the hookah?" she asked.

"It's pretty nice."

"How about you add a little hash to it?" She looked at me with a devilish look.

"What?" I said, caught off guard.

Esta took out a brown ball the size of a cockroach and handed it to me. I was surprised with the lack of discretion here. I had heard about drugs in Goa but had no experience with them.

"Put it in your hookah. It'll give it a kick," she said, smiling.

"What? Here?!" I said, wondering if the risk was really worth it.

"Yeah, just be discreet," she said, with encouragement.

I didn't know how discreet one could be, standing and putting hash in a hookah in the middle of a beach restaurant, but apparently it was no big deal. I took the ball and put in my pocket for later.

Esta was the DJ the following night and Dariush, my Iranian compatriot from the ashram, also was there. Another DJ was spinning and the music was like trance but slower and simpler. Ambient beats. People danced on the beach and inside the beach bar.

Dariush had just finished a session of Vipassana. I was curious because I was going there the following week.

"You know, Daria, it was great. But it was the hardest thing I've ever done."

"Okay, tell me more. How was the schedule?"

"It was rough. After several days, I would look in the mirror, unsure of whether I was dreaming or living a reality. Nothing felt real."

"Well, that doesn't sound so bad."

"I died and was reborn several times each day. You know *The Matrix*?"

"Yeah . . . "

"I felt like Neo but I was taking the red pill every day, countless times each day. It was hard. It's not for everyone but it feels good."

Just when I was hooked on what he was saying, he snapped me out of it.

"Want to go dance?" he asked.

"No."

I sat there taking in what he had said and considering its implications. Dayita worried about me doing Vipassana, saying that it might make me experience feelings I wasn't ready for, even after I related what Dariush told me. Esta overheard me telling Dayita how moved Dariush was by Vipassana and cut in, "He told me he hated it. He was telling me not to do it."

I looked around at the outdoor beach club, noticing in particular a group of young women and guys sitting next to each other. They all faced the dark beach, staring off into the distance. *Why aren't these people talking to each other? If I were any of these guys I'd be chatting up these ladies . . . ooooh! They're all stoned!*

It was a sudden revelation for me.

"Dayita! Dayita!" I took her out of her boring conversation with Dariush.

"Everyone here is stoned! Look at that group over—"

"Of course they're stoned!" she cut me off.

I looked over at her in surprise.

"Wait. So you knew?"

"Of course I knew! You didn't know?" she asked, bursting into laughter.

"Of course, why did you think I asked if you wanted to get a hookah when we first got here?" she said, smiling mischievously.

Slow on the uptake but better late than never, I realized the guy next to me was rolling a joint and the two men and two women sitting at a table across from me were zoned out completely.

*Fuck it*, I decided. Everybody is stoned. I started dancing like a stoner on the beach, only I was totally sober. I improvised a dance move that I think some of the stoners were digging. Pretty soon all of them caught on and copied my move. The whole beach was lined with a dozen kids all doing my improvised move. I felt like I was leading a Bollywood movie.

My euphoria was severely dampened the next day because Dayita was leaving. I would be completely alone for the first time in more than a month and I wasn't sure if I was ready for that. Staying true to my objective was constantly being tested, especially with a mother who talked to me every day for an hour, insistent on asking when I would return and indicating how much everyone wanted me home. Going back to the West was not yet an option because I knew my mind was not yet adequately prepared.

In the interim, I decided to use potato chips, ice cream, and movies as a distraction. Going out to satisfy my sugar fixation, I drowned out my thoughts with my iPod, swaying to the music in the street.

"Stop!" a guy jumped in front of me, shouting.

I looked up, startled.

*What is he looking at me for in such worry?*

I looked past him, some three feet ahead on the road. A long olive-shaped tube was writhing along. At the front of it was a head and a tongue that popped out every so often. I realized that this guy had just saved my life. Had he not stopped in front of me, I would have stepped right onto this five-foot cobra slithering along the road. I was so distracted by my music and thoughts that I couldn't even see in front of me. The venomous viper calmly made its way back into the jungle.

"It's a cobra. It is very dangerous," the man warned me of this obvious fact. I couldn't believe how close I had brushed against death.

The time had come for me to make the journey to my Vipanassa center in Saranath. In order to get there, I first had to stop at Varanasi, a perfect opportunity to tour one of India's most famous cities. Flying in India for the third time proved to be the charm as my flight was neither delayed nor canceled. I made it to Varanasi in no time (because I had slept the duration of four hours on two flights). On the second flight, the plane landed and I woke up to my neighbor tapping me on the shoulder. They were all deplaning and I was still asleep. I scurried to get all my belongings and walked to the front, saying my goodbyes to the flight attendants.

"Varanasi, right?"

"No, Varanasi is the next stop."

"Oh." I felt both embarrassed and relieved to have asked that question. I went back to my seat, where the woman two seats down continued to cry in her hands.

Arriving in Varanasi, I anticipated the small pleasure of not knowing where I would stay that night. I took the first taxi driver out the door, who was covered from head to toe in red and blue with a square Aladdin-like cap.

"Where you going?" he pressed me urgently.

"I need to find a hotel."

"Okay. Hotel, no problem."

"How much is it?"

"Today is Happy Holy, so 750 rupees." (or fifteen dollars.)

"No way!" I insisted.

"Okay. Okay. How much you want to pay?"

"500."

"Okay."

I felt like I was getting the hang of the bargaining thing when he brought me to the first hotel. It wasn't located by the Ganges River but he justified it by saying it was not far at all. He only wanted to collect his commission and leave. I told him to take me somewhere closer to the river, which he said would cost another 200 rupees. Now I started to feel like I was getting it shoved back in my face.

He took me to another hotel, still not by the river.

"There are no hotels by the river," he said.

Suspicious of the driver, I asked the bellhops about hotels on the river.

"Oh there are plenty on the river!" they answered in cascading unison.

I knew I wouldn't settle until I got the hotel I wanted. I asked the bellhop at the dilapidated hotel, which looked like it had been struck by war—and which the taxi driver had recommended—to find me a hotel by the river, which he did. Before going there, I was taken to one more hotel that was covered in tarp. As I stepped out to survey it, a four-year-old boy squatted and crapped right in the street in front of me. His mother watched on, making no fuss about it. The evidence of poverty and poor sanitary conditions shocked me. I was jolted severely as I realized North India was a whole new ballgame that would challenge me with many more curveballs.

The taxi driver finally took me to the hotel by the river and charged me yet another 200 rupees, but this spot—called the Palace on Ganges—was perfect. Not a five-star destination but it was classy and stylish in its own Indian way. The cherry wood and marble floors gave the appearance of a royal hotel. It was still pristine for its age and the rooms had large comfortable beds with high quality sheets. It was charming enough and I didn't care if it was overpriced. I bargained a little to get an extra 500 rupee discount and breakfast. I settled right in and ordered room service while watching NBA for the first time in a year. LeBron James was even better than I remembered . . .

~

The two main attractions in Varanasi are the *aarti* ceremony and a boat ride on the Ganges River at sunrise. I headed to the *ghat*, or pier, where the main *aarti* ceremony was taking place—one of the most popular sites for tourists from around the world. The holy Hindu ceremony involved five men performing various rituals as they waved candles, sparking flames, and goblets of fire in a dance under a moon that appeared more full and creamy beige than I had ever seen. The image was so prominent that I could make out the moon's craters with my naked eye.

The ceremony bored me after about twenty minutes of flames and dancing. I focused my attention on the throngs of Sadhus (holy men) wrapped in loin cloth, smoking some type of drug and then passing out, worry-free, on sheets placed along the piers. Sadhus, who often dedicate their lives to charitable works, fascinate the crowds. I've even heard of a Sadhu tying a stick to his penis and allowing people to stand on the stick. There were fires burning throughout the day, every day, for cremation and cows and goats ambling along calmly, as if their space amidst the tourist-packed piers was fully justified.

Walking along the piers in the dark, stepping as care- fully as possible, and using only the moonlight to guide me in avoiding the cow and goat shit, I became worried as I felt a young man following me. I slowed to see if it would affect his pace, and, sure enough, his brisk walk transformed to an aimless wander; when I stopped, he stopped. I had no idea why the guy was following me or what to expect. I mentally measured our comparable size, preparing to defend myself. My fists were ready. I would deliver the first and hardest blow.

I changed directions and slowed so often that the stalker finally grew impatient and left. Relieved to have lost him, I focused on my next task: getting to bed ASAP. I had a 5:30 AM wakeup call to catch the sunrise excursion on the Ganges.

~

This time, I wasn't getting screwed into paying more than I had to fork over. Price differences in India aren't set, so uninitiated tourists get the "let-me-screw-you-as-much-as-possible" rate. It gets overwhelming when thirty people rush you, trying to get you to rent their taxi. Once you agree to an acceptable "screw me" rate, you find that your day has just begun. You bargain on prices for food, for Internet usage, for a boat ride, and every other routine transaction. It becomes so exhausting that you don't even want leave the hotel. At least in the U.S., regardless of whether or not you're a tourist, you know what to expect in terms of price. In India, the lack of a set price sets up the expectation that everyone will try to screw over everybody else. At the end of the transaction, you get the sense that you got screwed. For example, as soon as I stepped out of the hotel, five men ran after me, asking if I wanted a ride. The same guy who had blown me off the night before because I refused to get ripped off came after me to make sure I had arrived at the intended location.

It was still somewhat dark as some tourists and I settled into an old wooden boat, which I expected to fall apart at any moment. As we rode along the Ganges, I witnessed the brilliant orange and pink sunrise turn into pure yellow as it rose higher into the sky with every passing minute. We stopped at the outdoor crematorium, where apparently hundreds of corpses are burned every day, and dozens more wait in local apartments for their death in order to be cremated in this location. I witnessed one body covered in a red cloth being dragged around on a gurney. The pile of ashes is an unforgettable sight.

*These are all the remains of dead people. And hundreds more are taking up shelter around the crematorium, waiting to die.*

It is hard to fathom living at a cemetery, looking at the inevitable final location of a body's remains. It is believed to be a holy rite to have one's ashes poured into the river because one is cleansed of bad karma in the Ganges and this liberates the soul into *nirvana*. However, children and holy men are not burned because they have little if no bad karma to answer for after their death. Their bodies are simply tossed into the Ganges after being weighed down by rocks. And, less than twenty feet away, old men and women are bathing and drinking the water, mothers are cleaning their saris, and kids are swimming around without a care, likely thinking, "Oh, that Prandu's grabbed my leg again! Always a joker, that one!"

On the way back, the day had commenced for the locals. They took their daily baths and swam. Kids swam to the boat, holding onto its edge and playing mischievously. People were happy and splashing without any troubled thoughts or concerns. They lived in such deep poverty, in a city that was so run down and filthy by most standards, and yet they still found something to smile about. Not only were they smiling, but they were laughing and looking completely content with life. They would wash their saris by hand, oblivious to the easier conveniences of electric washers, dryers, and laundromats. They didn't know any better about modern conveniences, but they also didn't care. They were perfectly content. More importantly, I couldn't help but wonder that in a world where we share so much—we see the same sun, breathe the same air, walk on the same earth, live with the same animals, and are bound by the same world and natural laws—that it is possible that lifestyles and beliefs can be so strikingly different. I might as well have been in another world. And for all intents and purposes, I was.

I arrived back to the hotel. It was my last free hours before the ten-day Vipassana program, where I would commit to a sustained period of silence. The prospect invigorated and frightened me simultaneously. I wondered if I could survive the wrath of the ego clinging on desperately for its life. It was comparable to claustrophobia. I had been warned about visions, hallucinations, and potential mental health issues, but my need for the experience of Vipassana was too strong.

## ⁓ 24 ⁓

I was about to spend the next ten days in prison—
actually, a mental institution. However, I was here
by choice. We pulled up to the imposing yellow gates
announcing Vipassana Meditation Center and the taxi
driver honked.

*Who would have anticipated the gates of hell being yellow?*

My nerves and depression took a turn for the worst
when I heard a man yell at my taxi driver in Hindi. The
driver turned around, facing me, and translated: "He says
you have to get out here, I cannot go in there."

Feeling like a condemned man, I said goodbye to
the driver and tipped him four dollars, the equivalent
of a tenth of his monthly salary, thinking perhaps one
more small act of goodwill might save me from what lay
behind those yellow gates. My driver was a rarity among
taxi operators in India. He kindly allowed me to use his
phone throughout the drive and never cajoled me into
paying him a higher fare.

This was my proving ground—the place where I
would dive into the depths of hell, the kind that only
exists in your mind. I had come to do battle with my mind
and, despite my anxieties, I reminded myself constantly
of the importance of remaining as levelheaded as possible
through this challenge. I knew my mind would prove to
be the biggest obstacle. However, despite knowing this, I

was about to be surprised. It's like knowing the ball will go to LeBron James in the last three seconds of the game but still not being able to stop him.

Walking to my home for the next eleven days, the fifteen-foot brick walls lined with barbed wire echoed the images of the concentration camps I visited in Europe. I never doubted my reason for visiting Vipassana; I only doubted whether I would make it. This was not a Hollywood-style ranch with all the amenities of a five-star hotel that attracted happy, contented individuals who said that they were spiritual and believed in spirituality. This was the real deal, that separated the ones who do the talk and those who really do the walk.

At Vipassana, one meditates for ten hours or more daily for ten consecutive days, never speaking to anyone. A similarly difficult task would be to dig to the earth's core—with a garden shovel.

The rooms were filthy with dirt that had accumulated over the years and the shower floor was a giant Petri dish of bacteria and mold, waiting for its next warm body. The shower was no more than a faucet with running water and a bucket. The toilet seat had been stripped of its original blue color—it had almost faded to white. There was evidence of rat droppings everywhere, and if that wasn't enough, bees had built a nest right outside the door and mosquitoes took over the room at night.

Fortunately, I had never been in prison, but I imagined that prison had to be better than this. At least in prison one could speak to others or read to escape the harshness of imprisonment. I recall seeing a documentary where one unlucky man "served" time in jail and in Vipassana. He explained that the latter was far more difficult because in prison one can bend the rules and eventually work them favorably. In Vipassana, there are no options for bargaining or for bending the rules. No materials for distraction or amusement are allowed—books, computers, writing materials, paper, pen, anything at all. In Vipassana, everyone has the same regimen—meditate, eat, sleep, walk, and think.

I didn't even have the benefit of secondhand experience from a friend or colleague.

Before going into silence, I met a Spanish guy with whom I shared my story about taking a dip in the Ganges River at Varanassi earlier that day. Retelling the story of how calming and liberating the experience had been, I was brutishly jolted back to reality when he said, "You know, in a bad river in India there are about ten thousand types of bacteria. In the Ganges, there are millions. With all the dead bodies, you also have to worry about leprosy."

The suggestive power of his words was immediate. All of a sudden I panicked and felt an itch in my groin. I thought that perhaps I had risked my health for a futile ritualistic experience.

And with that we headed straight into a room, the tension and nerves thick in the air. A relic of obsolete recording technology—a cassette tape—was played before we were told that Noble Silence would begin. No verbal or nonverbal communication at all. We were about to experience what it truly means to be alone.

Still unsettled by what the Spanish man said, I silently checked every physiological cue or signal in my body to see if any illness or disease was welling up. This was not the mindset I had expected prior to going into ten full days of silence. I worried about obsessing over what this man had said just before we began this extraordinary exercise of meditative discipline. I wanted to quit right away and go to a hospital for a checkup, but I listened reluctantly to an inner voice telling me to relax. I would come to rely exclusively on that inner voice. Only later would I begin to realize that that was the purpose of Vipassana and the essential nature of transformation.

After the meeting in which we started Noble Silence, all of us silently headed to the main hall to have our first hour of meditation. It seemed discouragingly difficult as my knees began to hurt from the sitting position. My mind wandered constantly back to the thought of how much time was left until I could get up and leave.

All night I couldn't sleep. My mosquito net was set too high to keep them out, giving them the opportunity to buzz incessantly in and around my ears. I became trigger-jumpy. In the middle of the night, I sprang up to the sound of a bell. Peeking outside, I was surprised to see it was still completely dark.

*This can't be right.*

A Russian man who had been randomly assigned to be my roommate and I washed our faces in silence and headed to the room with our floor blankets in tow. Hardly a flexible person, I knew that sitting cross-legged for five minutes would be the closest I would ever come to attempting gymnastics.

I closed my eyes and wandered off, trying to follow my breath.

*Breathe in, breathe out. Look at that breath, watch its nature. Oh shit, did I just feel an itch in my groin again? Oh no, that guy was right! I should never have dipped in that water. I am so stupid. How could I? I wonder what Mom will say. She will be so upset. My family will be so hurt and disappointed at my stupidity.*

*Wait, I'm supposed to observe my breath. Breathe in, breathe out, breathe in, breathe . . . I wonder how long it's been. It feels like thirty minutes but maybe realistically it's been only five. Damn, when will this be over? Can I make it through this thing? Should I just leave? Can I leave? I'm supposed to stay and they have all my stuff locked up. Breathe in, breathe out . . . besides, if I wanted to leave, I couldn't jump over the fence because of the barbed wire. All I really need is my credit card and passport . . . Oh shit, they have both of those! How stupid am I? Why did I give them that? Breathe in, breathe out . . .*

My mind continued to wander like this every few seconds, and it would take me several minutes before realizing how long my mind had wandered without my being aware. Somehow I made it through an hour and was proud of myself. Normally, I would have had a difficult time getting through forty minutes. Now all that remained was another hour of this session. However, I had made the fatal mistake: I had opened my eyes and looked at the time. The law is that once you look at time it goes much, much slower. But if you close your eyes for long enough you lose track and you have no idea how long it's been and you get lost. This proved to be a difficult lesson.

At least I had managed a few good moments of concentration. We had our vegetarian breakfast—mango, potatoes and curry, sprouts, chai tea—all fresh from the garden. Then we headed back for another round. Somehow the first day was over and so was my uncertainty about being able to survive. It wasn't so bad after all, despite a sore butt and the staff getting upset at me for taking an easy pose during the video lecture, which actually irritated me.

*Doesn't he know I've been sitting for ten hours?!*

The second day went by quickly as well. My concentration had slightly improved, and I was beginning to notice my mind had wandered off within a minute of it doing so. The days had an odd duality. Every hour of meditation seemed like eternal suffering but at the end of the day I wondered if it had really happened or if it was just a dream.

My concentration had improved dramatically the third day. I was so conscious of my mind at all times that it began asking for permission to wander. With firmer resolve, I would not allow it to for several minutes. I spent the entire two-hour morning session with my eyes closed and felt fantastic. The relief was short-lived when I remembered that a three-hour session was about to start. Again, I made it through the first hour, and there was some agitation and a lot of mind wandering during the second hour. But the last hour was utter mental torture from extreme boredom. Eventually, the bell rang and I was free. Once again, the relief was short-lived as I realized another session was about to begin and this time it would be four hours. And, after that, seven more days! My optimism was beginning to sag considerably.

This was going to be a lot harder than I thought. Each hour became an endless tug of war and by day seven, instead of having my mind asking permission to wander, I was begging it to focus for just one lousy minute. My imprisonment was complete.

When you don't know what you're getting into, you do not dread the pain because you don't know what to expect. You just deal with the pain as it comes, so you are only miserable during the actual experience of pain. When you know what you are getting yourself into, however, you suffer twice as much because you dread what is coming and make yourself miserable thinking about it. Then you are even more miserable during the torture because you made the issue that much larger in your mind.

At Vipassana, there was no break from the mind. I thought about skipping meditation but realized that I had nowhere to go and nothing to do.

*Where would I go? Back to my room and lay there and continue thinking? Walk around and continue thinking? After all, meditation is the realm of you and your mind. I'm not only meditating in the hall, I'm meditating all the time! I didn't sign up for this much meditation. I can't escape my own mind and yet I have lived with this my whole life. How have I lived with this thing for so long?*

As much as you might try rigorously to control your mind and thoughts, this will backfire, and your mind will start to rebel. Like an uncaged animal realizing it has the upper hand, the mind deploys its versatile and immense arsenal: disturbance, frustration, resentment, rebuke, anger, vengeance, and naked rage in an accelerating downward spiral. Hopelessness seems like a tempting option as you realize that there was no material incentive for doing this—nothing external to gain.

*Where's the incentive for sitting and trying so hard to meditate? Why exhaust and stress myself?*

I tried to relax, but it was only temporary as boredom returned, insistent upon uprooting all of my caged mental issues and deepest instabilities. It was a mental Armageddon, and I needed my strongest will to not lose it behind the gates of hell. My mind tantalized and teased me with smug, sardonic glee in the expectation that it could gain my total submission. Vipassana is not for those who do not understand the mind's deceptive tempting power and cannot deal with the battle.

Throughout the battle, I never doubted why I had come to such a place and why I had put myself through this. I only doubted whether I could make it. We were told at the outset that if we were there merely to play "intellectual games" and philosophize over life, misery, and the distractions of our cravings, then we did not need to submit to this torture. Those satisfied with just the illusion of the experience were told to "buy a video or listen to the audio lecture."

I came to realize how willpower is not to be confused with determination. In my opinion, determination is a state where one vows to overcome external factors to get to where he or she wants to be, but willpower is the vow to overcome the internal factors, which are far more formidable mountains to climb, in order to fulfill personal accomplishment. This battle is a stark solo event, where the consequences of failure can be destructive.

It was at once encouraging and distracting to have others there to share my misery. On the one hand, you could look to them for emotional support—just seeing that you were not the only one going through this helped. I don't know what it is about human nature, but the pain is lessened when we see others going through the same distress. On the other hand, the look of complete defeat on some of their faces could bring you down further. In my growing anger, my fellow meditators became the objects of my ire. The smallest cough felt like a slap in the face.

*How could this person be so loud? Doesn't he have any respect? We are meditating here!*

Occasionally, I would open my eyes and peek to see how bored others were, only to see that EVERYONE was in deep meditation. That would frustrate me even more. *I can't do this! These guys have practiced. They are cheating somehow. I'm not a hermit.*

We woke every morning at 4:00 AM to a morning bell. After a couple days, I would always be up two minutes before each bell. The bell would indicate the beginning of each mediation session and no matter what time of day I heard it, I always dreaded the sound. By 4:30 AM we were in the hall meditating until 6:30 AM. We would take a break to have breakfast and use the bathroom until 8:00 AM, and then meditate again until 11:00 AM. Then, we would eat lunch—all meals were vegetarian and all ingredients were from the garden in the ashram—and shower and sleep (it's amazing how tired I got from just sitting there) until 1:00 PM, and then meditate again until 5:00 PM. After, we could have tea, and because dinner was not served (to help promote quality sleep and meditation), we were given something similar to Rice Krispies cereal with peanuts in it. I tried one time to eat four bowls and the server eventually reprimanded me, saying that we were not to have more than two bowls max. At 6:00 PM we would meditate for another hour and, at 7:00 PM, a discourse was played on video for an hour and a half, followed by another thirty-minute meditation as a nightcap. The monotony was depressing and sleep was the only break from meditation.

Without the benefit of verbal communication, I had a chance to understand the Indian people. My conclusion is not flattering: They have very little respect for others, especially if you are a foreigner, and they always put themselves first. Standing in line to dry our silverware, the Indians would always jump in front of me and pretend I didn't exist. One came and squeezed himself in next to me when I was sitting at the end of the table. I looked around to find that every other table was completely open. He gestured that he was left-handed. He was so stuck on himself that he failed to see that I was left-handed, too.

In the meditation hall, I found other men were childish, constantly burping with their mouths wide open, yawning loudly like babies, with no care for the fact that everyone was meditating. Some would fart, others would sigh, and still others would snort all the snot in their nose up into their mouths with one ferocious inhale. However, the women stayed quiet except for one in the back who just didn't care. Looking like a cow, she wore saris that could barely cover the front half of her stomach, let alone the rolls of fat on her side. She snorted her snot, burping, farting, and making sounds as if she was licking a lollipop. Meanwhile, the Europeans, Japanese, and Americans didn't even make a peep.

By the fourth day, I started to feel vibrating sensations on my body that resonated with energizing excitement. *Am I stoned or crazy? What is going on here?*

As I discovered later, this was apparently a normal thing to experience. My concentration became deeper and deeper to the point where my breathing slowed to almost a complete stop, my heart was beating louder, and my senses had grown so sensitive that when someone would cough I would jump up in a panic, losing complete concentration as my heart was pounding. This became increasingly frustrating.

Later, I was curious to see how much people were struggling with the cross-legged seating position. Apparently,

I was the only one who struggled so much sitting. My thighs were feeling pulled beyond their capacity, then a sharp pain in my knees arose, and, finally, a deep soreness in my ankles.

*Why do they sit like this? In the West, we have things called chairs. Why do they suffer so much to sit like this? Why do I have to suffer like this? I am not Indian; I am not used to this kind of stuff and my body can't handle it. I must have a chair!*

Once again, the battle between agitation and relaxation needed to be squelched, but it was frustratingly difficult because I could not speak out or yell.

Luckily, the food was fantastic. We had fresh mangos and porridge for breakfast, a rice and peas concoction for lunch, and milk chai. This diet was essential to gaining a level-headed sense. I never felt too full; I never felt sick; I always felt light and sharp.

After two or three complete body observations in deep concentration my mind would be completely exhausted. My mind needed a few minutes' rest to just wander about idle things and, as a reward for its earnest cooperation, I would allow this.

On the afternoon of the fourth day, I laid in bed with my hands on my chest. I could feel energy flowing through my hands, a subtle, warm tingling in my face. I smiled with my eyes closed as I dozed off into a deep, restorative sleep. It was the natural and eternally satisfying alternative to Vicodin.

During the evening discourse, the guru would explain to us what we had gone through and its purpose, which helped to calm and inspire us for the following day. While the guru spoke to the collective group, I could not escape the sense that he was really just speaking to me. I listened to each of his words with more concentration than during my meditation. I realized that my meditation was evolving naturally on its own each day.

However, even on the seventh day, every time I marched down the long straightaway from my room to the meditation hall, I was anxious at a pin drop. Every time I heard the bell ring, the same feeling. One could peek under the crack of a door at the untamed stallion that was my mind, thrashing about in a locked room, but I knew that to tame the tricks of this beast, I would need to bring it out in the light. When the bell rang, I didn't agonize about what I was about to go through. I rose like a soldier and headed straight into the hall without wandering or taking the long route or thinking about it while sitting outside.

Walking around the square after evening tea, I started counting my steps around the square.

*Okay, so I have taken thirty-six steps and, if I assume that every two steps is a meter, that means I have walked eighteen meters which is about twenty, per side, which makes eighty around the whole thing and that means I need to walk around twelve and a half times to walk one kilometer. Okay, now if every mile is one point six kilometers then that makes . . . gee, why can't Americans switch to metric? It's so much easier. Those stubborn assholes are now making me do some hardcore calculations to find out how much I have walked.*

And like this the mind wandered from one subject to another. I did walk the whole kilometer, but it didn't feel like a kilometer, so I started to doubt my calculations. And there goes the mind again.

One day, after breakfast, I started thinking about the upcoming three hours and I decided to go on strike and not meditate.

*They can't make me meditate. I'm just going to stay in my room.*

And then another voice answered:

*You can't let your mind control you like that. You have to be strong and disciplined . . .*

*Okay, okay, I'll go in, but I won't meditate!*

I bargained with myself.

And that was my resolution. I went in the meditation hall and, after some time with my eyes shut, my mind craved to see what was going on and what time it was. I was so bound by time it was driving me insane.

*I will not look at the time. But I will just open my eyes and look around. NO!*

Before I knew it my eyes were open. Reality came back and I was no longer in the timeless blankness of my mind. I was back in life. And without noticing, I had also looked at the time! Fatal mistake. That's when the stallion kicked in and all hell broke loose. I could not control it.

*No more meditation. I cannot do this. How can they expect me to sit here for this long? They need to have stricter prerequisites and not allow idiots like me to just walk into hell without knowing it! I'm leaving! I can't sit here anymore!*

Outside, I felt a little relieved, but still not totally satisfied. I needed to get out of there. The worst part happened when I went back to the hall after lunch—I had skipped the rest of the thirty minutes of meditation. I sat down, somewhat calmed down from the morning's state of mind, and the teacher's voice emanated from the cassette player: "start again, start again." This irritated me so much more.

*How could the teacher have no understanding—no compassion? He is a guru with infinite patience and he can't understand what I am going through! How can he expect me to start again? I hate this guy, he is the worst guru and he is not even here! And the teacher sitting up there, the assistant, he doesn't know anything either. They are not enlightened, look at them! I have been meditating for five hours today and now four more! And then three more days on top of today!*

*Fuck this. I can't do it. I'm not a hermit. Only hermits and monks do this because they have nothing better to do. It's the easy lifestyle that they choose!*

I could hear myself laughing at my own insanity.

Frustration had turned to anger and it was burning up inside me. I couldn't hold it in. I had to find someone on the outside to blame. Someone to point the finger to— because clearly, I couldn't be the one at fault, or at least I thought so. My ego had caused me so much misery and I still couldn't help but associate with someone on the outside. I was intentionally walking into a ditch without a clue as to how deep it could be.

On the eighth day, I awoke with a renewed purpose, recognizing that it would be finished in three days. The meditation went quickly that day.

*Did the day go by or did I just dream it? Have I been here eight days or months? Who's to say I haven't been here for months? What is reality anyway? Is this life just a lifelong dream? Where does the line blur between dream and reality? Who is to say that anything we did in the past actually happened other than in our own minds?*

I had a mini-anxiety attack during lunch on the ninth day. I was taken over as it came up so fast and viciously that I did not have time to disassociate myself from it. It was me and I was it. It had taken over before I knew what had happened and, for a few seconds, it had subsumed me into a chokehold and I was ready to faint and fall. I was freaking out.

*What do I do?*

I panicked, thinking about getting up and heading straight to my room. Then I realized I had accidentally poured salt instead of sugar in my yogurt; instead of a really sweet yogurt, I got a small taste of the yogurt between all the salt. I had an idea to trick my mind. I convinced myself that the reason I was anxious was because I lacked salt, so I quickly ate it and convinced my mind that I felt better. I held onto this belief with all my mind and slowly the situation improved. I tricked it with a placebo.

When the tension built up and tried to take over, I knew I had to see it coming and prepare to get through it without getting caught in it. It's like a large wave crashing ashore, and one must learn to dive under and let it pass through. Knowing this was normal, I accepted it. Eventually I'd be able to calm down and continue on with life as if nothing happened. I was so far outside my comfort zone, the furthest I had ever been in my life, but maintaining discipline and finishing what I started was my main goal despite the despair and misery that had begun to take up permanent residence in my mind. The first six days, the devils popped their heads up and took a look around, but always went back inside through my pathways of control and stability. Eventually, they grew impatient and I had to grow more patient. Control was my objective as I observed them without reaction, without association.

I was missing the family and friends that I had been dead to for the past nine days, thinking of all the people I needed to get back in touch with, and imagining the first conversation I would have with my parents after I escaped. I played the scene in my head thousands of times. *What will be the first thing I will say to them after so long? What will their reaction be?*

I had never gone so long being out of touch with the world and, most importantly, my family.

I decided to walk outside. The light breeze brushed up against my face, which started tingling; the sun was setting—a perfect prelude to a complete clarity of mind. Things became so clear, with so many signs I had been given on this trip and prior to starting. I just could not link them together: so many goals and thoughts had become so obvious. Every piece of the puzzle fell into its rightful place. It was as if I had spent my life putting the puzzle together piece by piece and now I could step back and see how they actually fit. The future was clear and unattached to any particular result, and I understood that the wheels just needed to be set in motion; the rest would be taken care of by an assured power outside my control.

Once all of this became clear, I just started running. I decided to run around the square for as long as I felt was enough. All the listless, seemingly lifeless individuals looked up at me, their expressions saying it all:

*Where is this energy coming from so late in the game? Has he gone mad? Is he pulling a Forrest Gump? Have we lost him?*

But I just didn't care at this point. It's funny how well one gets to know people without words, as so much communication is transmitted through body, gestures, and eyes. Silent actions and movements can tell no lies.

I woke up on the tenth day pissed again, insistent that this experience was now over. After about forty minutes in morning meditation, my stubbornness won out, compelling me to go back to sleep. I left the hall, dozed off in my bed, and moved through the ether into a beautiful dream where I played the guitar and jammed with a pianist and another guitarist. The euphoric melody captivated us when the dream was rudely interrupted by thumping raps on the door. I jumped up to open the door to a tall Indian man dressed in white robes who stood there looking at me like a father catching his son selling drugs. To me, sleep was a drug and as far as I was concerned, I was the biggest drug dealer of them all.

"Will you please return to the Dhamma hall and continue your meditation?"

I was shocked by his courtesy. I was ready to unleash ten days of anger on him, but his courtesy left me no other option.

After our final meditation session ended at 10:00 AM, the head guru finally allowed us to speak. In a magical instant, the tension and the pressure built up during the last ten days dissipated.

"So that's what 235 hours feels like," were my first words.

The seemingly neverending story had ended. Everyone was ecstatic, like prisoners released from jail. As I looked around, I saw nothing but the biggest smiles I had seen in more than ten days light up the faces in the room. Pure joy resonated as I felt an understood bond among us that was as strong as family. The bond was like what I think combat veterans share—the unspoken acknowledgment of a joint experience in hell too deep and implicit to explain fully to anyone. The bond grew deeper as we understood that we had shared our greatest moments of desperation—without an uttered word.

~

I packed my bags and though I was happy to leave, I was not as excited as I had imagined. Though I had replayed this day in my mind at least a thousand times, the anticipated emotion wasn't there. However, there was something. It wasn't excitement to leave the center, but rather a joy to celebrate the gratefulness of joining the world again. Free from my prison, I could actively participate in the world again. The grass was greener, the trees more durable, and the people that much more kind-hearted. Daily routines were a blessing, such as the capacity to bargain with the taxi drivers, check my emails, and speak to my friends and family after so long. I had so much to say about having done nothing for ten days. More to say, I would imagine, than someone who had participated in the familiar game of life for ten days.

I told my best friend about the hell I had sustained and I could hear his mother in the background.

"Tell Daria to stay away from these kinds of things. He needs to watch out," she warned. The comment amused me, and I felt like a patient, wise father watching his child struggle with reading the first time.

Even the rough beauty I had failed to see before revealed itself—the mud huts, vendors napping on their hammocks on the side of the road, and cows roaming the countryside without a care. I was feeling a sense of gratitude that I had never experienced before—holy, magical, and indescribable—and I was profoundly moved to tears.

The theory of Vipassana suggests that misery arises out of craving and aversion. With the practice of Vipassana, neutrality and acceptance of situations settle in and bring about an immovable peace in all situations. I had to go through hell to see that the world is heaven in comparison and that I had been blind to its beauty all along. Though neutrality sounds simple, it is the hardest lesson to incorporate into our daily lives—to enact when emotions and deep-rooted desires sway us.

I believe that we are not victims of continual reincarnation as Buddhism suggests, but it is our choice to be reincarnated because of the experiences we wish to have in life. We arrive in this world to experience life as we choose it until we are ready for the next experience. Through this, we move upward in our evolution as humans and spirits. It is not that misery traps us. Instead, we choose misery until we have evolved enough to navigate our own path for further development. And, until one chooses to move beyond, the person cannot be forced. Rather, the individual must continue to experience his current state. Karma, as many see it, functions to instill fear for its personal, instructive purpose. However, karma runs much deeper than what one does to others will come back to the individual. Actually, we choose our karma on a much deeper level and as we treat others in a certain way, we experience it simultaneously ourselves. When one experiences the feeling of giving a person something he or she desires, the happiness the receiver has is matched if not exceeded by the giver's happiness. And in this way, karma is instantaneous.

~

At the Delhi airport, Dayita and I reconnected, but she did not recognize me immediately. I had lost ten pounds in a mere ten days and had grown a full beard. I had gone incognito.

## ⤳ 26 ⤶

Dayita had arranged for a driver—a young, plump, quiet man—to take us on the twelve-hour trip to Dharamsala. I didn't know exactly why I wanted to go to Dharamsala other than the fact that the Dalai Lama's temple was there (which wasn't even much of a motivation as he himself may not have been there and I'm not one who particularly enjoys seeing different temples). There was a deeper intangible reason, but all I knew was that the urge was strong and I trusted it. Traveling abroad on long road trips changes one's perspective on time. A three-hour drive from San Francisco to Tahoe that once seemed daunting would now seem like a walk across the street.

My new sensory appreciation was intact as I viewed the mysterious trees, hiding the secret understanding of life and its corollary wisdom. I could actually see the trees' beauty for the first time as the essential metaphor for humans: their elegant branches, the vibrant leaves, and their majestic stance in the captivating sunset. They understood the complex balance as they patiently waited for us to discover it. As I looked out on the open sky with my head in Dayita's lap, I spontaneously blurted out, "We should go camping. I want to get lost among the stars."

"Yeah, we can do that if you want. There are probably some places along the way where we could camp," she said with the businesslike demeanor of a well-organized tour guide.

We stopped for a brief respite at a hotel resembling a seedy brothel where only the most desperate go for relief and entertainment. The walls were pockmarked with chipped paint, pieces of asbestos had fallen from the ceiling to the floor like giant snowflakes, and it seemed obvious that the blankets and pillows had not been washed for years. There were food stains and God knows what else on the pillows, and the toilet wouldn't flush. We had no other choice but to sleep there for the night. I crept in bed, blocking out every unpleasantness, and closed my eyes until the next morning.

At 7:00 AM the next morning, Dayita and I were more than ready to reach our destination and, with only a straight shot through Punjab into Dharamsala, we left. Our driver, who had been a paragon of kindness and patience, had had enough when we reached the city. He simply wanted to drop us off on the street corner and make his way back. After twelve hours of driving, it was hard to believe that he couldn't spare an extra ten minutes to help us find suitable accommodations.

The Dalai Lama's municipality reaches high into the Kangra Valley, surrounded by a dense blanket of conifers. One can readily see the snow-capped Himalayan peaks. Here, everyone was Tibetan, monks were omnipresent, and every other person was wrapped in red robes with a shaved head. Immediately, Dayita assumed her role as a Tibetan, bowing to certain monks and watching them closely as they assessed her for escorting a non-Tibetan.

We drove by several hotels, unsatisfied. We continued our search until, finally, it was unmistakable.

"This is it," I said, as déjà vu settled over me. The vision I had in the Vipassana ashram was realized right in front of me. The mountainside view, the floor-to-ceiling windows, the green trees, the hardwood floor, the vantage point for mountain viewing—all of it was there. I had brought myself to my dream without knowing it.

Once I got to the room, I went to take a shower and realized the hot water wasn't working.

"Sir, please wait for fifteen minutes," the front desk operator said.

I waited for twenty minutes and called again.

"Sir, please wait for ten or fifteen minutes." Again, I complied.

I ended up waiting most of the day, and finally I called, in an extremely angry tone.

"Sir, please wait for about . . . "

"I have already waited all day and every time I call you say wait another ten minutes!"

"Okay, sir, I will send the boy down."

I felt victorious.

"You see, Dayita, when you cause a scene you get your way. They could have sent the boy down the whole time but waited until I was upset to send him down."

The boy came down, took a look in the toilet, and turned the knobs. After a one-minute inspection he concluded, "It's going to be another ten or fifteen minutes."

My anger was useless. I gave up. The water would come when the water would come.

I didn't shower that night.

# ~ 27 ~

Dayita and I spent our last two nights in Delhi at her sister's apartment. Luckily, I was no longer bothered by the cockroaches that scampered unashamedly around the bathroom floor.

Back in a large urban metropolis, I did what many Americans like to do: I went to a mall. We took the customary rickshaw to the newest mall in Delhi. I was at once relieved and surprised to see something so modern in a country where all I had seen was evidence of a society entrenched in backward mode. The shops brought me back to the U.S., where Lacoste and Burberry, Nike and Adidas lined the three-story mall. I felt underdressed for the first time in India, but I had nothing better to wear. I walked by the retail facades, picking out my favorite pair of Nike shoes that I hoped to buy upon my return, my preferred Lacoste shirt, and, before I knew it, I was an American again. I returned to the consumerist mentality I had strayed away from for so long. Funny how quickly one can fall back into the same routines.

We decided to see the film *The Book of Eli.*

"Sir, would you like gold club tickets or regular?" the man behind the counter asked.

"What is gold club?"

"You get certain privileges."

"Such as . . . ?"

"The seats recline with leg rests, you have a private viewing, you get access to a menu of food; the theater has fewer people."

Eager to sample an opportunity that was not available in the U.S., we thought about trying it, but then decided against it because we would have to see the film later. It was ironic that in India one could experience going to a movie theater with gold club privileges.

For our last night together, Dayita and I decided to put together a grand feast from the mall's offerings. We ordered Tandoori chicken and kabobs from one stand, Tandoori chicken sandwiches from another, and pasta from a third vendor. Clearly, we weren't able to eat it all, but I did gorge like a glutton. Dayita and I didn't speak. The quiet yet impending end hung over us like the shadow of death. She was going to lose me forever and the thought of it left her uncharacteristically detached. I tried to ignore it, suggesting we go to the Häagen-Dazs store for a chocolate chip cookie sundae.

"Sure, if that is what you want," Dayita responded in a sad tone, almost as if she was giving a cancer patient his last wish.

The absurd size of the sundae broke the darkness for us as we gobbled up this mega-concoction, leaving our stomachs screeching in pain. The meal shocked my digestive system, now habituated to light, vegetarian meals.

I went through my bag, remembering the perfume that Amelie gave me in Mongolia. At the time, I was thinking:

*What the hell am I gonna do with perfume?*

Now, it was clear why that perfume had traveled with me for six months. It was destined for Dayita. Dayita was ecstatic about the gift. She had scoured India looking for that exact fragrance, which came from France and was difficult to obtain abroad. No act is ever inconsequential enough to deny its significance.

~

The airport goodbye was difficult and emotional for me. I knew that once my luggage was checked in, I could not leave the airport entrance. However, we did not expect that Dayita would not be admitted. Stuck between the exit and the entrance and the two sets of sliding doors, we gazed at each other for a long time. Two armed guards awkwardly stood between Dayita and me, forcing our goodbye to be quicker and less emotional than we had anticipated. The goodbye would have been difficult as it was, but now, with the stony gaze of two armed officers as spectators, it seemed more like a visitor's time in prison. Without making a scene of it, we both said our hurried goodbyes, summing up a two-month journey together in less than two minutes.

At least I had the less-than-stellar timeliness of the Indian airlines to ease the immediate emotional void I was experiencing. Despite their regular schedules, Indian airlines clearly struggle to master the concept of on-time departure. Of the seven flights I had made in and around India, four had been delayed and one was cancelled, and this last one was no exception. It was delayed by an hour.

*What would these guys do if God forbid there was less-than-perfect weather conditions, like clouds, wind, or even, dare I say it, rain?*

After an hour up in the air, distracted by the onboard entertainment, I didn't realize until the second announcement that the flight was turning back toward

Delhi because of a crack in the runway at the Kathmandu airport. No other information was offered to passengers. We returned to Delhi and sat in the airplane for about an hour until it resumed the flight. Magically, the crack had disappeared from the runway and we could now land there. A journey that should have taken no more than three hours total took longer than a transatlantic flight.

Despite these material annoyances, I was anxious to begin the experience in Nepal, alone yet again for my final destination.

~

# PART FIVE

*Nepal: Gratitude in Unexpected Places*

~

## 28

Upon entering the airport in Nepal, I realized the visa process would be as much a pain as it was in Bali. With more than a hundred passengers, it would take well over an hour to process all of them, and we had to fill out forms and give passport photos. I had to exchange money. The officials accepted U.S. dollars but, unfortunately, I had no American cash on hand and the man at the money exchange counter was more than willing to screw me over with my traveler's checks. He charged me once to exchange my money from dollars to Nepal rupees and then yet more fees to exchange them back to dollars so that the visa processing counter would accept my money. It happened so quickly and I didn't want to end up at the end of the line, so I just took the money and ran. It was too late. I was already the last person in line.

I was the last one out and the only bag left was mine. At the prepaid taxi stand was a fat man wearing a Hawaiian shirt and asking far too many questions.

"Where are you from?"

"America."

"Ohhhh, America! Where are you going?"

"Hotel Vaishali."

"Okay, friend, you like to chill out?"

"What?" My unsettled mood suddenly became that much more unsettled.

"You like to chill out?" He looked deeply into my eyes, his behavior seeming strange—actually scary—in many ways. How would the others be?

"No, I'm here for a specific reason and don't have time for anything else," I answered in a brisk, chopped tone.

"For what? Buddhism?"

"Yes."

"Okay, here is my card, call me if you need *anything*," the strange man said, placing unmistakable emphasis on that last word.

I was relieved to escape but I didn't know what looked shadier—the guy or the taxi I entered. The car appeared to be at least thirty-five years old and looked as if it was going to fall apart on the spot. There was no radio—at least in India the taxis had radios—the speedometer didn't work, and the suspension obviously had given up long ago. There were no seatbelts, which proved to be a shame because every bump in the road sent me flying into the air. The driver didn't say a word to me the entire trip. He simply drove through dark alleys and streets occupied by blocks and blocks of dilapidated buildings and a few people walking here and there. I thought that at any moment he would stop and invite his friends to mug me, knowing I was an American and probably had money.

After what felt like a never-ending terrifying ride, I made it to supposedly one of the nicer hotels in Kathmandu and checked into my room. I was not surprised when it didn't feel like a four-star hotel, much less a one-star destination where a Travelocity recommendation would definitely have been suspect for its authenticity. The lobby was old and dilapidated, and the ugly terra cotta floors and low ceilings accentuated the cramped, depressing ambience. After a long, exhausting day, I didn't want to be awake for another second, so I dozed off until morning.

The next day, I went to the lobby to get a cab and see the monk whom Hamid and Dayita had mentioned. The man at the front desk took me to another table and started negotiating with me.

"We can give you a luxury private car for the three hours for two thousand or three thousand rupees." I expected a Toyota sedan from the current decade or something similar, but he pointed to a car outside that was unrecognizable. I'm sure most car companies would deny ever having made it. The car looked to be from the 1960s or 1970s.

"That's the luxury car!?"

"Yes, sir," he said, completely matter of fact.

This place is a joke.

## 29

"Where are you from?" the *rinpoche*, sitting on his throne, asked in an intimidating tone. Nearly bald, wearing glasses and dressed in red robes with yellow lining, this neat, short, frail man reminded me of the Tibetan version of the Mahatma.

"America. I have been told to come see you."

"You are depressed." He handed me a large pear.

"Umm . . . no . . . no . . . I'm not depressed," I stammered.

"Stop crying. Don't cry. Here take this." He poured some black pellets in my hand and I just looked at the peculiar mass.

"Eat it!" He announced. I picked some up with my fingers and looked at them.

"Eat all of it." He gestured, instructing me to lick all of it from my palm.

"How long are you here for?" he continued.

"As long as it takes."

"Come back later."

"When?"

"Tomorrow, lunch time. Noon. Now sit! Meditate!"

I was flabbergasted at being taken completely out of my element without any indication whatsoever. I was confused, lost, dreaming.

*How did I get here? Who is this guy? Am I depressed? I'm not depressed.*

I couldn't understand what he meant saying I was depressed. Moments before we spoke, I had never been happier in life, believing I was finally figuring things out. That implied that I have gotten nowhere. I was beginning to think perhaps he meant that I was depressed merely as a temporary state since I had left India and Dayita and, once again, I was alone in a new setting.

Dumbfounded, I tried to make sense out of this hellish situation. However, the overheard chants gradually calmed me and transported me to a different realm. I realized that I had blinded myself from seeing my true core over the course of this journey. No matter how hard I had tried to come into contact with my deeper being, I just couldn't see it. Now, I saw how I had been urged to come here, how this inner being had carried me, knowing every moment precisely what needed to be accomplished. Then I imagined the seemingly conscious "dumb me" who had no idea, an entity walking here and there and, at times, fighting the inner origin of my knowledge. The "dumb me" merely had accomplished the objective of stopping my "inner me" from genuine progress. With stunning clarity, I knew just how blind I had been to myself.

This comprehensible core was external to my mind. My mind, in all its efforts, does not have the capability to understand the soul, which knows where to push. Meanwhile, the mind reads and tries to rationalize this concept of soul, but real understanding lies outside the logical realm of comprehension where books and teachings cannot complete this mission of full understanding. I saw how tirelessly it had worked to bring me to the point where I would stand speechless in front of this man, where my mind would not work, because my soul was doing all the talking. My mind was on pause and since then it had remained on pause. Absent of goals, without ambition or motivation to go anywhere, it was just sitting there unsure of what to do in the next moment. For the first time, I began to see how I engaged myself with my soul.

The glimpse was momentary but yet strong enough to transform my perception of understanding. All these books and words come and go but can never actually show you what you have to see yourself.

I remained seated, wanting to make sure the *rinpoche* saw that I had not left. After the ceremony, I headed for lunch, a nice vegetarian meal that I gobbled quickly. Afterwards, I thought it would be better to leave and wait until the next day.

"He told me I'm depressed!" I told Dayita over the phone. She was the first one I called and she didn't know what to make of it either.

"You know, they all work in different ways. Don't preoccupy yourself with what he said. Just wait and see what happens. Go with your heart." Her words seemed so genuine and filled with love. I listened and took a nap as soon as we ended our call.

I went out to pizza that night. After getting lost around town, following the receptionist's directions, I finally found the place with the help of a bicyclist trolley man. It was my first time sitting in a restaurant alone in a couple months, and I didn't miss the feeling.

The surrounding scene was curiously romantic in a cheesy way, with couples at three candlelit tables going through the universal moves of dating and love. The music—all sappy, lovey-dovey emotional ballads of lost and found love—capped the scene. I ordered too much: a pizza and a side order of focaccia. I didn't eat it all because I didn't want to be a gluttonous sinner so I thought: *Why not just box this and give it to a homeless person or dog on the way?*

*No, where will you find a homeless person at this time? Give it to a dog? Are you serious? Besides, this is Nepal. They probably don't even have boxes for the pizza.*

This seemingly logical exchange in my mind, however, gave way to a new voice:

*Don't worry, the person will appear. Just make the effort.*

So I asked the waiter for a box and, to my delight, he asked if I wanted one box or two. Then I walked in the street, looking around for a homeless person. After a few minutes, I spotted a man who appeared to be getting ready for sleep on the bare sidewalk.

"My friend, are you hungry?"

He nodded and I gave him the box. I walked away without another word. There was no other person in the street for the rest of my walk to the hotel.

*Yes, I thought all along that this concept of the universe giving you everything you need was nice. I believed it to an extent. But I saw it actually work, quickly and precisely with my cooperation in making a gift from the pizza. Deep down, I expected the situation not to work out, and assumed I would live my life half ignoring the truth. But the truth was too blatant to ignore. The universe did not fail me. It worked according to plan. It was there to allow me to experience and realize that it is not just something in my head, a construct of perception and mind, but, instead, an ever-present force manifesting itself in real, natural ways.*

The discovery was frightening in its empowerment and the implications it carried. You must simply be aware.

I woke up tired as hell, unable to leave my bed, and worried about the things I had to do.

The small breakfast room, where tablecloths were rarely washed and cups were usually dirty, was closed, but I squeezed in and got what I needed before they took away the food from the buffet. Then I spoke to the manager, Kamal.

"I want to extend my stay so can you give me a single room? I don't need a suite."

With barely a pause, he told the receptionists to find me a room.

"How much is a single room?"

"It is seventy dollars for you since you are a valued customer."

*My ass, the suite was eighty-six dollars . . .*

"The suite was eighty-six dollars, that's ridiculous," I protested.

"Yes, but you booked through an agent [it was Expedia] so you got a good rate. Normally, we charge ninety dollars for a single room."

Of course this was ludicrous, because the best hotels in Kathmandu charge between one hundred and one hundred forty dollars with new furnishings, better facilities, and a much less depressing ambiance.

"No, for that much I will not take the room. It's okay. Just check me out," I said in my most serious business tone.

"How much you want to pay, sir?"

"For a single room here . . . fifty dollars."

"Okay. No problem."

Getting a huge discount proved to be surprisingly easy.

I went and found my taxi driver and we headed off to the monastery. I went straight to the room where the *rinpoche* sat across a table from a man.

He studied me for a moment. "Where are you from?" Then he added, "U.S."

"Yes."

"What is your question?"

"I just want to tell you why I'm here."

He smiled knowingly as if it didn't matter what I had to tell him. It was obviously foolish to share my story. He already knew me and what I came for and what I needed. Words were not required. However, the *rinpoche* entertained my desire and told me to sit.

My nerves kicked in and I had that peculiar anxious feeling of unexpected and monumental change, of walking a path with no clear return. I had waited since I was sixteen for this moment—to be here in a monastery, learning from the source of Buddhism and to hear the untainted message, pure and sweet like a melody. My hands were shaking and my heart was racing.

*Will I make it out of here? Will he take me in? Will I like what I learn? I have already lost motivation; will I gain it back or live forever in emptiness?*

Suddenly, I wanted to leave and go home. But then I recalled how much I had gone through and how I had come out on top, realizing that every challenge was worth the effort to arrive at this destination.

*I must be strong. Relax.*

Meanwhile, he dealt with a middle-aged Nepalese man who pulled out a large wooden blue and pink dragon mask. The *rinpoche* was delighted to see it. I waited a little longer and he ordered the monks to bring me a drink.

After the the man left, the *rinpoche* approached me. "What is your question?"

"Uhhh . . . " I was dumbfounded again. I just wanted to tell him a story.

He left without me answering and went into another room with the man who had the dragon mask. While he was gone, two books written in English were placed on the table. I finally understood this man's objective, which was clear from the instant he met me. He had noted the irrelevance of asking the question. It didn't matter much what I had to say. He had a plan. He came outside and told me to read the books and return when I finished. As I prepared to leave, as dumbfounded as on the previous day, he looked at me and asked, "You look like Saddam Hussein's son. Where you from, Iraq?"

"No, my parents are from Iran."

"I knew it."

"*Rinpoche*, I have a question. Why did you tell me I was depressed and not to cry when I wasn't crying?"

"You were. Even now you want to cry, look at your eyes! I can see it. I know what you want. Don't worry."

He stood there and tapped repeatedly at my chest with his knuckles. He wanted to lighten me up. He grabbed my head and I just stood there, unsure.

"You are taller than me. Lower your head." Then, he whispered, "You are confused. I can help you, my child." He kissed me on the head.

The *rinpoche* released me and then looked into my eyes once more. Again, he grabbed my head, lowered it, and kissed it. I felt safe, secure, accepted. All my wishes and desires had been placed in his acceptance of me and I had passed. My feelings were indescribable—a mix of happiness, peace, relief, calm, and that fundamental feeling of having been moved through my depths. His words were only a small part of what he had done. His energy was what moved me through his interaction, piercing my body and seeing straight into my soul. He saw my kindness and my genuineness and enjoyed it.

He handed me a package of some type of fruity cake, chocolate sticks, and an orange.

"You see this man . . . " he said, pointing to a monk dressed completely in maroon-colored clothing. "This man can make you laugh. Just look at him and laugh. Talk to him. I am a busy man. Come back later, I have an interview now."

He invited me to be happy; to get out of my funk. I don't know where the funk or sadness had come from but somehow it had surfaced in all its starkness.

I went outside and the monk in maroon robes came out and sat next to me.

"You don't want to talk to me. Hold on, I will get someone for you."

I hadn't said a word and he just left. He came back with another younger man.

"This is lama Oser." Like the others, Oser had shaved his head and was dressed in red robes. Somewhat chubby with a warm smile and bright eyes, he was kind and attentive when he sat next to me. I poured my heart out to him, told him about getting the *rinpoche*'s name from two people I had met on this journey, and about how I had wanted to be here ever since I was fifteen.

"Have you told the *rinpoche* this?"

"No. I haven't even gotten a chance to speak to him."

The *rinpoche* came out and the *lama* went in the room with him. The *lama* returned outside and resumed our discussion. The *rinpoche* wanted my chat with the *lama* to continue uninterrupted.

I continued, sharing the details of my life and how I consistently felt empty. I told him of the visions from the previous day, along with the story of the pizza and the homeless man. While telling it, I felt that maybe this story seemed insignificant, meaningless. I mentioned that this is just a small example but it means a lot to me. He was intrigued by this comment.

"How long have you been like this? Seeing these little things?"

I didn't get a chance to answer when he was disrupted by a woman who brought us a simple but appetizing vegetarian meal that included rice, boiled vegetables, and soup.

"You know I am lucky to be with you. I usually don't get this kind of good food. You must be a special guy," the *lama* said.

"I'm glad I can help, even if it is unintentional."

We spoke for another forty-five minutes before he had to leave.

"Do as the *rinpoche* told you. Read the book and come back." He left without saying another word.

I sat alone with a bunch of food, cakes, a chocolate stick, an orange, and two books. All alone. I finished my food and left, helping an old woman up the stairs as I departed.

I woke up remembering a dream where the Dalai Lama came to me dressed in a suit and jumped onto tall ledges like Spider-Man. He was terrifically agile, moving nimbly as if he were a young man. His priority was to make me laugh.

With a relaxing day ahead, I decided it was time to shave my beard. The local barber managed to add a massage.

Despite what I read in the book the *rinpoche* gave me, the essence of its teaching seemed frustratingly elusive. I felt as if I had lost motivation, a nightmare from which I couldn't escape. Nothing made me laugh much; I had lost that invigorating zest for life. I simply felt dead and I didn't care about anything.

*How could this* rinpoche *give me these books without telling me anything or giving me instructions? Why do I feel like this?*

Anxiety intensified my fear for not feeling anything.

*What if I go crazy and am just dead like this my whole life? What if I go insane? Who am I?*

I had lost my mind, literally—certainly everything familiar. The depression was deep. My mind had been uprooted and all kinds of negative emotions kept arising strongly, swaying me about like whiplash in a high-impact car crash. Overwhelmed, I wanted to do something drastic.

I wanted to go back to my old way of life. Speaking to Dayita convinced me otherwise, at least temporarily. "You have already crossed the line. There is no going back. You have your feet in two boats, and it is causing you worry. Just let go. Just trust it. These feelings will continue and you must be strong. They will get worse," she said.

Terrified, I forced myself to sleep.

## ⪢ 32 ⪡

I woke up in the morning, this time with a different dream: the *rinpoche* told me to reread the book he had given me. I didn't put much significance to this dream because I was going to see him.

After breakfast, I found my driver and we headed to the monastery. I arrived before the ceremony had finished so I waited before going to the *rinpoche's* chamber. The line was long and many Nepalese people came and cut in front. I waited in line. Ahead of me was a young American girl. I didn't pay much attention to her as I was so focused on what I needed to get from the *rinpoche*.

Finally, after many children, Americans, Germans, and monks had their turn being blessed, I had reached the *rinpoche*.

"Did you read the book?"

"Yes."

"What did you think? You don't believe it?"

"I do. It's just that I'm confused. What am I feeling? What did you give me? Nothing matters for me. I just don't care about anything and I'm scared."

"Don't be scared. You are facing reality. Don't think. Come here."

He grabbed my head and tapped me on the head with a ritualistic object covered in an artistically embroidered silk cloth.

"Stay here. Talk to the people here. Talk to the *lama*. You will be okay."

The monk I was told to laugh at previously escorted me out and I sat outside. Feeling more cheery, I was smiling, not as dark as when I had arrived at the monastery. The monk introduced me to an American monk, who sat and listened to me. I explained how confused I felt.

"This is quite normal. I felt the same way. It is the way you deal with it that matters. Here is a precious gift that has been given to you, and you can go off the deep end and leave or you can stick around and try to learn."

As we were in the middle of our discussion, the funny monk came out and called me back inside. I went inside and the *rinpoche* had a pamphlet in his hand.

"Take this. Sit down."

The pamphlet was titled *Why Feel Renunciation*. He knew how I felt exactly. I thought the key to my success out of this slump was in that pamphlet.

There were four cushions on the ground with wooden tables in front of them. On each was a bowl of vegetable soup along with a plate of assorted potatoes, carrots, and onions with rice and meat. I sat in the only available cushion next to the American girl.

"Why you come to Nepal?" the *rinpoche* asked me.

"When I was fifteen, I lost faith in God. No one could answer my questions except for one teacher of mine who was a Buddhist. Since then, I have wanted to come to Nepal. I have been on a journey for eight months, and met two people, one in Mongolia and a Tibetan girl in India, who gave me your name and told me to see you. That's why I'm here. And now you have given me something in the past couple of days and I don't know what it is. I just have no motivation. I feel dead."

"Not dead. Frozen," he said, pausing for a moment before continuing.

"Don't be afraid. Your mind is not sharp. But you are a very fortunate person. You are lucky to be so fortunate. You need—some people have mind—not so sharp, like you. Like a knife that cannot cut paper, but some people have mind so sharp, it can cut other metals. Where you from?"

"San Francisco."

"I'm going to San Francisco. Why you come all this way to see me!? I'm coming there!"

"When will you be in San Francisco?"

"July or August. He has a center there," the American girl interjected, replying on his behalf.

"Your mom or dad from Iran?" the *rinpoche* continued.

"Both."

"Ahhhh . . . "

"What does your mother and father believe? What religion?"

"My father, no religion, no beliefs. My mother is spiritual."

"Like what spiritual?"

"Like New Age spirituality."

"Ahhh . . . "

After lunch, the *rinpoche* got up for his next set of interviews.

"Help this boy. He is alone. Take care of him. He needs a friend to open up," he told the American girl.

Then he looked at me.

"Open up your heart."

He stopped before walking out the door and looked at me again.

"I know what you feel. You have a culture shock and also *Dharma* is simple, but complex. The message of *Dharma* is simple, but the techniques are hard."

"I have no techniques."

"Stay here and learn. Speak to other monks and people. Stay here will be good for you." He turned to the American girl again.

"Take care of this boy. This boy is very good for you."

"I will," she replied.

"You understand he is very good for you?"

Then he turned to me. "You understand?"

"No, my mind is not sharp." I looked at him and smiled. "Come here."

He opened up his arms wide and I walked into them. He gave me a big hug and rubbed my back.

"You will be okay."

As I walked back, he turned to me and said, "You are afraid of her. You want to stay away from her. Give her a hug."

Both the girl and I were embarrassed, as the subliminal sexual tension between us had been exposed. We didn't know what to make of this situation. We couldn't hide anything from this man. In fact, he knew things we weren't aware of and he wasn't about beating around the bush. I did as I was told and gave her a hug.

"How old are you?" he asked me.

"Twenty-two."

"How old are you?" he asked the girl.

"Thirty-two."

"Very good. Perfect. You are young; she will make you grow up and he will make you young. He is very good for you."

And with that he walked off.

The girl gave me her number and told me that if I was interested she could find me a place to stay nearby. I had been staying about a thirty-minute drive from the monastery.

"I have a friend who has nice guesthouses. Let me call him. I can show you the place today or tomorrow. Actually, just call me around five."

"Okay."

I walked off.

I headed back to the place where the taxi driver had parked and couldn't find him. I sat on his car and waited for half an hour and read the pamphlet. Nothing of substance was in there. Nothing new. Nothing real.

*What does he mean I don't have a sharp mind? I went to the best private high school in my area, maintained a fantastic grade point average, and went to one of the top universities in the U.S.*

*Is he trying to get me out of my mind?*

*Does he know how much value I place on this mind and so he wants to shake my confidence?*

*Is he just trying to confuse me?*

I decided to head back to the monastery. I found the driver sitting there, waiting for me.

## 33

"You can only fall victim to such influences if you allow yourself."

On the phone, my mom did not disguise her concern.

"You had made this guy such a big deal in your head and you allowed him to make you completely vulnerable."

Upset that the *rinpoche* might have taken control of her vulnerable son, she could not bear to see me endure this pain. My mother was eager to give me a piece of her mind despite understanding the reasons why I had decided to make this journey. Her loving bribe offering Persian kabobs did not make it any easier.

"It's been eight months, just come back! That's enough! We are all tired of this!"

*They can't stand it anymore? How do they think I feel? Coming from all that comfort and luxury? If they are tired, then I must be exhausted. But I won't quit.*

I returned to the monastery but the *rinpoche* was busy with the last day of *puja*, a daily series of Buddhist rituals and chants that culminates in a festival celebration at the end. Meanwhile, I talked to a woman from Iran who apparently knew Vipassana. "Be careful. There are people who have gone crazy and come back completely different. Not human, not normal."

"Well, were those people happy?" My question apparently caught her off guard.

Some people, I'm sure, might be vulnerable to hysteria following an experience like Vipassana, but I was completely confident that my search for genuine happiness did not carry those risks.

Leaving the monastery, I stopped at the market and bought a box of Trix cereal, Oreos, and Reese's chocolate. I was desperate for anything that could transport me to the comfort of home.

I spent the rest of the day in solitude, meditating and not speaking much to others. I picked up a book by Osho, an Indian spiritual master whose New Age-style writings often unsettled conservative figures in Hindu and Buddhist religions. In one of his books, which remind many Americans of figures such as Eckhart Tolle, a phrase immediately leapt out at me:

"When you come to a master to surrender . . . the ego creates all sorts of difficulties, rationalizations not to surrender: 'think about it, brood about it, be clever about it.' When you come to a master, again the ego becomes suspicious, doubtful, creates anxiety. Again you are coming to life, to a flame where death will also be as much alive as life."

## 34

The first few days with the *rinpoche* had thrown me for a loop. Expecting feelings of happiness, peace, and newfound wisdom, I was instead caught off guard as he pelted me with echoes of my deepest demons. Now, I had returned to a stable state. In fact, I was much like my old normal judgmental self, often thinking enviously about cash and tricked out cars.

I went to the restaurant for breakfast, carrying my box of Trix cereal. I just didn't care what people would think. I sat down, filled a bowl with heaps of tiny artificially colored corn products, and added the restaurant's milk. It was the treat I was hoping for that day.

I walked to the monastery and headed upstairs to where the *rinpoche* usually ate lunch. The cook who had served me once before recognized me and mumbled to me in broken English that he would be back in an hour and that I should have lunch.

Unsure if I correctly understood the cook, I went to the office and spotted a book about Dzogchen. The staff invited me to take the book, along with another, so I went out to the back of the monastery where a huge tent was set up for lunch. I sat and waited.

After about two hours of waiting and lots of silent judgmental observing, the *rinpoche* finally appeared.

He was there with other high-ranking incarnations—including one who was no more than fifteen years old and another who could have easily passed for a six-year-old boy. They wore orange shirts under their robes while the *rinpoche* wore dark yellow.

There were more than one hundred people who were planning on having lunch with the *rinpoche* and these other monks. I made eye contact with the *rinpoche* several times. He always knew whether I was there or not, even in the crowd. I always felt watched, like he was assessing me. Lunch was over and he invited whoever wanted to come up.

I ran up there and when my turn came up, the *rinpoche* paused. He looked around and talked to the others, telling them to clean the table. Meanwhile, another man—a short burly Nepalese guy wearing a white collared shirt and jeans—jumped in for a blessing as if his life depended on it and got a hard slap on the top of the head. Finally, after a couple of minutes, the *rinpoche* turned to me.

"How are you feeling today?"

"Back to normal. It's all gone."

"This is a good sign. Now you have real peace. You are now my family, we love you, everyone here."

"*Rinpoche*, I want to learn the techniques I can use for life . . ."

"Come to my teaching Saturday!"

"Can I come tomorrow to see you?"

"Tomorrow I am gone. Come Saturday."

The nature of the student-teacher relationship in this realm is difficult to understand, even for those who experience it. There is no curriculum; one doesn't even know what will happen or what will be given. You just sit there and allow your energies or souls to do the exchange.

In the end you leave, not knowing what you picked up in that exchange. Afterward, you are more attuned to your internal emotions, aware of subtle cues that would be barely perceptible to any outsider. It was funny—maybe even ludicrous—to think that I had come all this way just to have a seemingly minor exchange with the *rinpoche* for no more than two or three minutes each day.

The man is so busy with all his commitments and at times it seems that he doesn't have time for you, but when you are in his presence, his entire attention is focused on you and everything else fades away. He could embarrass you in front of hundreds of people by screaming something aloud but you just wouldn't care.

After the exchange, I waited for the taxi, fully pleased with the day's events.

On the phone, Dayita listened without interrupting me.

"I think what I felt the first few days were just my innermost obstacles; my deepest fears surfacing. It was like Vipassana but much more intense, as I felt that these were tsunamis and earthquakes shaking me on the inside rather than aftershocks. Either he brought them out of me and now I have been cleared by some of my deepest impurities, or I was just tested."

I paused for a moment, looking to hear some affirmation from Dayita. She said, "Yes, the hardest part is the initiation, the beginning. You made it through and you will experience something new every day—some days up, some days down—but it sounds like the difficult part is over. I know the feeling. You felt like the ground was taken out from underneath you. You are lost; you don't know what you know, and you don't know anything. You feel nothing inside. It is the essence of emptiness that you felt. You saw the truth."

"So what happens next? Is it over? Does he have more to give me?"

"It's never over. You should continue going to him and just be around him. Don't rush it. You know people train years and years to experience what you did in one week. You must have very good karma to have been ready for such a thing. Don't worry. The next thing will come when the time is right, just be patient. He might take you deeper. Now your mind is more calm and comfortable than the first few days with the move and the loneliness."

The phone call ended and I was still replaying Dayita's words in my mind later when I checked my email. Dayita had sent me a message:

*Till now you entrusted your Self to be guided by your own higher Self to bring you where you are now: to read the books which would eventually build a certain understanding of what you are looking to pursue, and to be with people who would guide you further to where you are meant to be. Your whole journey til now was preparing you for what you are to move into now; you may realize at certain times the importance and purpose of everything small and insignificant that happened to you and how the universe has worked so hard in detail to be able to put you where you are now; in fact sometimes you may just find some of the answers to your questions in some event or words you came across before.*

*I am aware that you already are familiar with its workings, and I only hope that you would let the nature of the universe take its course and meanwhile just have faith that along the way you will discover more fathoms of peace, wisdom, and contentment once the initial hesitations and dilemmas fade away . . . and until then you have to remember that you are not alone and you'll have angels manifesting in human forms who would contribute immensely through various ways to assist in your path to personal illumination . . .*

*Your acceptance of the rinpoche by acknowledging the effect of his energy on the depths of your soul, and his inherent ability to spark your inner vision and manifest the essence of your nature which is predominantly kind and compassionate, (examples of which I witnessed at times when your heart lay heavy on your mind) has already led you to the process of mystical initiation into realization of your own higher self.*

*Love,*

*Dayita*

~

I headed toward the *thangka* shop to meet Prabind, a local vendor about my age I had met while looking at his paintings, for some tea. He was a twenty-four-year-old Nepali citizen running a family business selling Tibetan and Buddhist paintings, also known as *thangkas*. I had gone to his store plenty of times, each visit looking at the same painting—of the white Tara goddess sitting in the lotus position atop a lotus flower. The painting was striking in its use of brown, black, and golden hues. Tara had three eyes: one between her eyebrows, another on the forehead, and the third on her right palm. Wearing a half crown with embedded jewels, she was joined by three deities above her, with the Buddha in the center with yet four more deities. I debated about whether or not I should buy it.

"Hello." Prabind appeared behind me almost as if by magic.

"Hey, you came out of nowhere!"

"Come inside. You want some tea?"

"Sure."

"Black or milk?"

"Milk."

We sat in the comfortably sized, well-lit back room of his small shop and he pulled out my favorite paintings again, for at least the twentieth time in four days. I started looking at them again. They were *thangkas* of Buddha, Tara, and all sorts of other deities. While many of them were traditional representational works, some were more abstract for how they depicted multiple layers of life and death.

"You know, it sucks that you guys don't have power most of the day," I told Prabind.

"Yes. We have many problems here in Nepal. Our life is very difficult."

His emotions started to bubble up.

"You know, my family had a very difficult time. Now we are better but before, you know, my dad died when I was two years old. Then, my uncles are educated and they took our land and my mom is uneducated. We had a very difficult time living. My brothers had to work and now they have this shop. I didn't finish school and went to Goa to sell garments. But now, things are better."

I was a little unsure of where this was coming from and why he had become so worked up emotionally. Prabind had always seemed to be quite calm and in control of his emotions. However, as touched as I was by his story, there was nothing I could do but to give him a comforting and understanding smile, which apparently seemed enough for him.

"You want to come to my village?"

"Sure."

"My village is very different from here. You will be surprised."

"Yeah, I experienced the same thing in Mongolia. Like you get water from a well and you have cows?"

"Yes. We have a well in our house and I have a goat and buffalo . . . I will introduce you to them." He looked at me and smiled. I couldn't stop laughing at that comment. We both got a kick out of it. We drank our tea and continued chatting about life.

## ⇒ 35 ⇐

I headed to the monastery to listen to the *rinpoche*'s teachings. Cushions were laid on top of rugs on the monastery floor for our comfort. As soon as he arrived, every person in the crowd of one hundred-plus people jumped up, and as he sat, everyone bowed reverentially, except me. I didn't see the point to bowing to this man out of a blind need to follow the herd. In fact and unfortunately, I felt that most probably didn't know why they were bowing; not only that, but by unquestioningly following something without really understanding it, they were missing the whole essence of whatever they were trying to seek.

The talks were nothing new; the concepts were all familiar. Renunciation stood out for me, but not in the sense that we leave our material society to live a simple life. Instead, it is to renounce everything that causes us misery. Renunciation is a refusal to participate in the disturbing emotions of anger, anxiety, jealousy, pride, and all the other negative emotions arising from clinging to the ego and believing it to be our genuine essence.

After the talks, which lasted about an hour, I waited in line to see the *rinpoche*. He smiled warmly, grabbed me behind the head, and pulled me close to him for a heartfelt hug and a kiss on the head. He put a red thread around me and tied two knots around it.

"How do you feel today?"

"Great!"

"Good."

"*Rinpoche*, when do you have more time for me to just come and hang out with you?"

"Come to Europe."

"No, I can't do that, but I will go to your center in northern California in July."

"Okay, good. We can go swimming."

"Yeah? You like swimming?"

"Yes. We have a river in our center, I put my feet inside."

"I have a swimming pool at my house if you would like to come for tea and a swim."

"Yeah? Where you live?"

"Well, I have a place in Sonoma and one near San Francisco. Whichever you want."

"Yeah? Okay."

And with that he moved on to the next person in line. My time was up.

I headed to Prabind's shop, where he was waiting for me.

"You ready?" he asked me.

"Yes."

We started walking and I stopped to ask, "How much is a taxi there?"

"250 rupees." This was about $3.50 in U.S. currency.

"Okay, let's get a taxi."

"No, you will ride the bus and get the local Nepali experience."

There was no way out, and I was pushed outside my comfort zone again. We walked out of the tourist part of town and entered the more polluted part of town. All kinds of trash littered the sides of the street, with cows going through it and flies all over. There were fruit peels, cartons of drinks, plastic—pretty much anything—and some of it had been burned to the point where one could no longer tell what it was.

We stopped at the corner of a busy intersection where white vans were queued up.

"Is this the bus stop?"

"Yes. That's our bus," Prabind said in a matter-of-fact tone.

The bus was a long white van with five rows of seats and everyone squeezed in on top of each other. The three-inch space I was given to sit on was a just little less comfortable than getting driven around by Tyson, the local taxi driver. However, the ride only cost us ten rupees.

A young man kept the van's sliding door open constantly, yelling at local pedestrians. He directed cocky comments at the guys and flirtatious calls at the women. Many passengers were local shopkeepers going home; some were mothers with children on their laps. The van stopped on random street corners or at any arbitrary point where passengers would hop aboard. Technically, the van was never full. The motto seemed to be: Let as many onboard as will fit themselves into the van.

"Why is he yelling at all the people?" I asked.

"He is asking if they want to get on the bus."

"Why?"

"There is no fixed bus stop. He picks up as many as he can along the way."

At one stop, a Nepali lady stood outside with an enormous sack that she could not have carried there alone. She entered and the young man put her sack inside.

"What's in that sack?" I asked Prabind.

He spoke to the lady and asked her.

"It's grains—probably chicken food."

The answer amused me and my face must have really communicated this because the woman looked at me and started laughing.

We got to the end of the road and started walking toward Prabind's house, passing through his village, a veritable ghost town of maybe a few hundred huts. The main square was completely deserted. It could have been a production set for the Discovery Channel's *Life After Human* series. The houses, on the other hand, were not too shabby. They were newly built with fresh paint, with some going as high as three stories. While a five-year-old in a kindergarten art class could have easily picked many of the bright and terribly matched colors, the houses actually looked like they had been expertly built. However, dilapidated brick houses also were scattered throughout the neighborhood. Prabind pointed to a small brick shack, telling me that his house was similar.

We walked through the empty town somewhat reminiscent of a Western movie backlot where a shootout could occur between the only two people living in an otherwise deserted area. Prabind showed me the temple he went to every Saturday as well as the local school, which looked like a mud house jail, complete with the barred windows. Prabind told me that tuition cost the equivalent of fifty dollars per year and even so, most kids could not afford it. However, Prabind was lucky enough to have the experience of schooling.

After about half an hour of walking, we arrived at his house, which was brick on the outside and mud on the inside. His room measured no more than eight feet by eight feet and the ceiling was less than six feet high. The ceiling was lined with cardboard because the mud would sometimes crack and fall. Looking through his barred window, I saw a cow poking his head inside.

"Is that your cow?"

"No, that's the neighbor's," Prabind said, obviously entertained by my reaction to his place, which apparently I did not hide well enough.

"Is that your closet?" I said, pointing to a line of eight nails in the wall from which two pairs of jeans and four dress shirts hung.

"Yeah," he laughed.

I couldn't help but think about how crammed my backpack was with clothes and how I kept lugging it around even though I was trying to travel "light." Here was a guy who really did live lightly and didn't think much of it. While I might have been amused by Prabind's humble surroundings, I actually envied the uncomplicated simplicity that was attached to them.

We sat with his sister-in-law and drank milk tea. We toured his house, where twelve people lived, including four brothers and their wives, his mother and sister, and several goats. His room was the smallest of all, and once served as the chicken coop. His brothers had a much larger room with nicer sheets and furniture. Prabind lived the simplest of them all. His aunt was dressed in thin red rags of a traditional Nepalese style, brown sandals, and a long ankle-length skirt, while his sister-in-law was dressed more contemporarily with t-shirt and long khakis.

They had their own well outside, along with an outhouse. Around the back there was the buffalo's barn lined with overlapping circles of animal feces on all four sides.

"Why do you have so much poop in the poor buffalo's house?"

"We use it for fire, to cook," he smiled at me. "You see that building there? That's a chicken farm. My plan is to have one someday and after that my family will be okay. We will be making good money and won't struggle anymore. And you see down there? That's my buffalo grazing."

I was impressed by his positive sense of motivation. He pointed out a parcel of barren land once used for agriculture. Now it showed some signs of development.

"You see, this used to be a field where we would play football. I mean soccer. Now, it has been built on and the field can't be used. And beyond this, you can see that whole valley down there used to be empty; now it is full of houses. They are destroying the nature and putting houses."

It was a sad sight, similar to what I saw back home in subdivision after subdivision of cookie-cutter houses with no distinguishing characteristics.

"So Prabind, where do you go to hang out with your friends and girls? Is there a village hangout spot?"

"You see, in my village and in Nepal, the girls cannot go out, not even with their friends. They have to stay at home. I do not see my friends because I am busy every day with work."

"So, is there a local cutie that you like?"

"What?"

"Is there a girl you have had your eye on?"

"Yes, she is very beautiful. The most beautiful girl in the village but she has a boyfriend I think. Probably in the next year or two years, I have to get married. My family will find me a woman and I will be married like my brothers."

"So why don't you try to marry this girl that you like?"

"She would not marry me. We have never even spoken. I have just seen her."

"So are you a virgin?"

"Yes," Prabind said hesitantly.

"Even after having had a girlfriend for four years?"

"Yes."

"Jeez, that is torture. I would never last that long in a relationship with no sex."

Prabind laughed, definitely embarrassed at this comment.

"You know, maybe we have a problem in our society," I told Prabind. "We plan all our free time around sex. We buy sexy clothes, go to clubs, and drink a lot so that ultimately we can meet a girl and have sex. Our life revolves around it."

"That is better than Nepal," Prabind said, half-jokingly.

I pointed to a used condom on the ground. It was an unexpected discovery.

"Prabind, they do have secret sex here!"

"Yes, sometimes they do."

"How come you didn't do it with your girlfriend?"

"Even if we have secret sex, if maybe my family finds out, they will be very upset. Also, I would have to marry that girl; it would be very bad for our reputation. Even if a girl is caught smoking a cigarette, the village will not like her."

"Is there like a caste system for marriage?"

"Yes."

"Can a beautiful girl move up in the caste system?"

"No. If she marries a man in a higher caste, they would have to run away. Neither family would accept them."

Hearing this reinforced my appreciation for the liberties back home. In fact, I felt more than a little guilty for not appreciating fully my privileges in the U.S.

I reached into my pocket, remembering my phone that I had brought to give away.

"Here Prabind, I want you to have this. Put your SIM card in it and see if it works. If it does, you can keep the phone under one condition: you have to give your old phone to the girl who works next to Lotsman's store."

"Okay," he said, like a teenager who had been given an unexpected present by a parent.

Prabind had always been reserved, careful not to reveal too much emotion. Giving him the phone, I felt a lightness—a distinct aura of happiness arising from him. It was a small gesture of goodness but I could see that, at that moment—at least temporarily—he was enjoying blissful satisfaction.

"There is a soccer match I want to watch but I don't know what time it is and we have no power."

"Let's go to my hotel room and watch it," I suggested.

We headed back to Thamel, making it back in time to see the last ten minutes of the game.

## 36

Today was the last day of my solitude. Dayita was coming to see me again. I waited around until it was time to go pick her up and, as expected, her flight was delayed by two hours. At the airport, I waited at the exit for more than an hour and she was the last one to exit the plane.

Happy to be reunited, we sat in the back of the car with her head resting on my shoulder. Tyson, of course, was the ever-obliging chauffeur. She was quite surprised with Kathmandu.

"I didn't know it was this bad," she said with clear disappointment.

"Yeah, it's pretty bad."

"So much pollution—look at how old this car is."

She watched Tyson pump the gas pedal as he switched on the ignition to start up the jalopy.

"Is that really how he turns it on?!" she laughed at the effort Tyson was exerting.

There were the customary piles of burning trash. It was a culture shock for her, coming from India, the country where most Westerners typically get the shock of their lives. She immediately comprehended the level of my reaction when I arrived in Nepal.

In Thamel, we went straight to the shop owned by the local scarf vendor, Lotsman. Unfortunately, Lotsman was sad today because of his brother's unwillingness to see him. Before I knew it, Dayita was lecturing him in Hindi. He had tears in his eyes.

"Dayita, he's not ready to let go."

"No, he is. He will feel better. Give him a hug."

"Lotsman, you have a good heart. You are a good man."

He just looked at me, depressed and hopeless as ever.

Meanwhile, the young woman next door noticed Dayita's presence immediately.

"Is this your girlfriend? Very beautiful!" she said with clear envy in her voice.

"No, I am his sister," Dayita said assertively.

"Oh . . . " the young woman was slightly relieved but still half hesitant to believe Dayita.

Shiva, the hat vendor, was excited to see Dayita. So was his boss and a couple other guys.

"Is that your girlfriend?" they asked.

"Yes."

"Oh, good. You introduce?"

"Sure, come on."

The guys were like hungry wolves that had set their eyes on fresh meat. They could barely keep themselves from becoming drooling fools—a simultaneously amusing and shocking sight. When Shiva was introduced to Dayita, he stood there speechless before asking a couple of general small talk questions.

We then made our way to Prabind's shop, where Dayita scrutinized every little detail of every *thangka*. Her father used to make thangkas and she would help him as a little girl. I was impressed with the depth of her knowledge. Meanwhile, poor Prabind was being grilled on the quality of his paintings, like a senior art student who was being examined by the faculty before graduation.

"This is not a traditional Tibetan thangka. We would never use such colors. Is this gold plating even real? It is supposed to shine much more than this!"

She paused, as if waiting for Prabind to answer, but she barreled right along.

"How much are you selling this for? It shouldn't be more than . . . "

Prabind looked like a cornered cat. Every flaw in his work was exposed and it looked as though he had never been so vulnerable.

Dayita eviscerated him in five minutes, long enough for any exit to be awkward. When we finally decided to leave, we walked back down the now quiet streets of Thamel. All the shops were closed and the atmosphere was always ominous at this time. We entered the half-closed gates of the hotel as security watched us closely. He followed behind us and as we got the key and made our way up the stairs, the man at the front desk yelled, "Sir, excuse me! Sir! Come here!"

I looked down and knew what had happened. The security had informed the front desk that I was with Dayita. The problem was that they had thought that I had brought a local Nepalese prostitute back with me. Because sex is not allowed unless one is married, they did not want me to break the law in their hotel and on top of that, I had only paid for one person in the room. I had already warned the manager that Dayita was coming. Unfortunately, his only advice was to sneak her upstairs.

"Come back!" the front desk man kept yelling at me.

I went up to him.

"What is the problem?" I asked him.

"What is your room number?"

"2124."

"When did you check in?"

"Two weeks ago. Listen, this woman is not a local Nepalese girl. She is my friend from India."

From what I could make out, the front desk man told the security to nab Dayita. My anger boiled up quickly and I was ready to rip the man's head off should the situation escalate. He had crossed the line in degrading Dayita and I was beyond furious. There are only two women that I would be so protective of that I would let go of any logic or reason and allow my reptilian instincts take over: my mother and Dayita.

"WHO THE HELL DO YOU THINK YOU ARE? HUH? YOU THINK YOU HAVE THE RIGHT TO YELL AT ME TO COME OVER HERE DOWN THE STAIRS LIKE THAT? YOU THINK I AM YOUR SLAVE?"

The confrontation had invigorated me tremendously. I felt like the Hulk and the man now was definitely unsettled and nervous.

"No sir, I didn't mean . . . "

"LISTEN, I HAVE BEEN A CUSTOMER HERE FOR TWO WEEKS AND YOU THINK YOU CAN JUST TALK TO ME LIKE THIS?"

"Sir, I wasn't . . . "

"YOU NEVER EVER TALK TO ME LIKE THAT AGAIN. IS THAT UNDERSTOOD?"

"Okay, sir."

The man was terrified and he made no effort to argue. Rightly so, as I probably would have grabbed him by his tie and punched him with no apologies.

"Now, if you have any problems, I have already spoken to your manager about this. Go speak to him and don't ever talk to me again."

"Sir, I am sorry for . . . "

I cut him off again by walking off, ignoring his words. I never heard from him again.

Back in the room, my body was still shaking. The only other time I had reacted like this happened when my mom was insulted at a restaurant. Every layer of peace and calm control had been shed, revealing an angry core.

The next morning we walked to the lobby and saw my favorite employee, a young, athletic, good-looking man who had transferred all of Dayita's calls to my room. Normally, he seemed mature and reserved, but like others who had met Dayita, he melted into a giddy boy trying to impress this attractive woman. He spoke to her in Hindi, asking the standard questions anyone asks when they are introduced. However, he quickly moved from common courtesies to probing personal questions for Dayita so I grabbed her hand, thanked the man, and dashed out the door.

The next day was Saturday and, as usual, the rinpoche was giving a teaching. Dayita did not want to go to the monastery for fear of running into people she knew. Apparently, news had spread like wildfire among the Tibetan community that Dayita was with a man in Dharamsala. The last thing she wanted was more gossip. Instead she wanted to go take care of a few ritualistic things at the stuppa (pronounced stoop-ahh), a gigantic dome-shaped chunk of rock with religious significance.

I told Dayita to follow me and instead of taking her to the stuppa, I took her straight to the monastery. So she sat at the back and waited for the rinpoche to appear. I decided to wait outside, where the air, relative to the monastery, was fresh and easier to breathe.

I ran into Lama Oser and we spoke for a few minutes. He asked me about how I felt and I recounted my improvements since our first meeting. I told him that I wanted to learn proper meditation and he advised me of the critical essence of having the right guidance. He remained intentionally vague, saying that improper meditation can be ineffective and harmful.

Mid-conversation, the *rinpoche* appeared and all chatter ceased. Everyone bowed heads and as he walked, he would stop and touch some people on their heads, bless them, and speak to newcomers. He walked past me without noticing and after speaking to a new individual, he walked back and grabbed my arm gently.

"How are you feeling today?"

"Great."

"Come, come with me." He led me into the monastery where he began teaching.

After the teaching was finished, he opened it to questions. In front of me, two young American women were sitting—one with a straight back in the lotus position (or Indian style, as we call it in the U.S.) and the other typing away on her laptop. The two, pretentious in their newfound passion for Buddhism, obviously used it as a tool to raise themselves above "ignorant Westerners." It was patently evident in every gesture they made. They would laugh extra loud when the *rinpoche* would speak in Tibetan, bluntly displaying their miniscule understanding of Tibetan to all, and scoffing at any Westerner who asked a question. They wanted to fit in so bad that they rejected and looked down upon their own Western culture. I was amazed to see such haughty women so desperately following a religion that aimed to rid one of the confines of the ego. In all their sophistication and class, they had missed the whole essence. This was the real tragedy.

When I returned to Dayita, I saw that one of the Spanish men sitting in front of her was flirting. Dayita later said that he passed her a note in the middle of the lecture asking what her name was. A few moments later, a young *rinpoche*, whose name literally means "precious one," spoke in Tibetan with Dayita. It seemed as though she was getting the inside scoop on everything at the monastery—who to see, where to go, knowledge they don't give to Westerners. She was immediately hooked into the social scene there. I left to speak to my *rinpoche*.

"How are you?" he asked me.

"I'm great, *rinpoche*. I went to Tulku, the man you told me to speak to, and the abbot at Kopan and he told me that I should learn meditation from you."

"Why did he say that?"

"I don't know. Can you teach me?"

"Yes, when I get back from Europe I will have more time. Also in America, come to my class."

"Okay. Will you come to my house for tea? I would like to gather some close friends to meet you."

"Yes. Speak to Kathy and give your information and I will come."

He introduced me to an American woman who was guarded about giving me any information at all, as if I was a kidnapper and the *rinpoche* was her son. She gave me the name of his center in California.

"I know of his center in California. I need his information so he can come to my house for tea."

"I don't know his schedule. His schedule is unclear and busy; his coming to America is a long time from now! I don't know what he wants me to give you."

"He said to give me his email or some way to get in touch with him. If you don't know what to do, just go ask him."

"He is busy now."

Eventually she gave me her email address and told me to contact her but I knew that in a few months time, this woman would again refuse to offer any help. I looked over to the *rinpoche* and saw him speaking to Dayita. He stood and walked out with Dayita behind him.

"Follow me," she mouthed silently.

As we walked up the stairs to his room she explained the conversation to me.

"He was classmates with one of my uncles, grew up with another and knows my whole family. He was also very happy to see a Tibetan attend his lecture. He told me to follow him up to his room."

Little did she know that I went to his room every single time, invited or not, and would try with only extremely limited success to chat him up.

We crashed a party, or rather a gathering, that the *rinpoche* was having, with about thirty students he had taught for the year, consisting almost entirely of Westerners. Afterward, as Dayita spoke with the *rinpoche*, I spoke to Buchung, the funny monk.

"Where were you? I didn't hear from you all week!"

"Well, my friend came and I've been busy."

He looked over at Dayita sitting next to the *rinpoche* and suddenly a knowing smile came to his face.

"Buchung, I was supposed to get *rinpoche's* information so he can come over to my house in America."

He took me to another room and gave me the *rinpoche's* driver's cell number and his own. He also showed me the *rinpoche's* detailed schedule, which Kathy (the obstructionist at the office) said was nonexistent.

"Call the driver and if there are any problems, call me."
Dayita came up to us with two pamphlets in hand.
One I already had, and the other was about meditation.

"Meditation! I have been going around asking all
these people about proper meditation and he just gives
you the pamphlet like that!" I said, my voice sounding a
bit frustrated and angry.

"Yeah, I mean, I guess so."

"Give me that," I yanked it from her hands.

"I guess he gave me the pamphlet so that you would
read it," Dayita joked.

On our way down, we ran into the young *rinpoche*
and he walked with us. Again, he and Dayita spoke in
Tibetan and I just followed along quietly. I felt like the
third wheel and the guy just would not stop talking—as
if in his whole life he had trained in incessant speaking
rather than meditation. He obviously was hoping to wear
her down enough that she'd be motivated to leave me.
While I wasn't jealous, I could see he couldn't comprehend why Dayita would be hanging out with a foreigner
instead of a well-heeled young *rinpoche*. His efforts to
impress Dayita were futile because Dayita had witnessed
this behavior many times before. However, she did not
want to be rude so she humored him while I stood by as
an essentially helpless bystander.

I later found out that he was bragging about his lin-
eage and status and asking Dayita about hers. A *rinpoche*
enjoyed an elevated status above other monks, not that
different from a prince who had born into power and status. He invited us to lunch. He was simply not fased by
the fact that Dayita was with me and he did not acknowledge my presence at first. We sat for lunch and he started
showing me pictures in his phone, among which were a
Ferrari and a picture of Will Smith.

"Ferrari! Ferrari? I thought you are a monk! You aren't supposed to be after these sorts of things."

He explained to Dayita in Tibetan and she translated.

"He says that he recognizes the essence of physical objects as emptiness."

"What a pile of shit! So you're saying that if I gave him a Ferrari, he wouldn't be ecstatic?"

Again, after some translation, Dayita explained his answer.

"He says he would be half happy, half sad. Happy that he has that thing, but unhappy because he recognizes its essence as emptiness."

There was nothing I could do but laugh. I was staring at a fraud in costume. Some "precious one."

We headed to the *stuppa* so that Dayita could light some candles. Buddhists believe that lighting the candles illuminates the darkness in an individual's journey to seek enlightenment. Obviously, lighting the darkness costs about ten rupees per candle and one must light them in increments of 108 in order to get the benefit. So, Dayita decided to do 216. I asked her about it while she was lighting them and a younger *rinpoche* who was in love with Dayita told me to come outside. He warned that I should not speak to her while she was lighting the candles because she had to focus. Immediately afterward, he spoke to her in Tibetan, rambling on much as the young "precious one" did. True to previous form, the young *rinpoche* tried to intervene between the two of us, suggesting that it was a matter of appealing to her sense of culture. However, much of this seemed like opportunistic nonsense and challenged my prevailing ideas of what it meant to be on a spiritually pure path of enlightenment. Guidance is simply that—guidance—and there are no absolutes. Guidance furthers our own understanding of what we want, not what they tell us is true.

We headed to a shrine where they did a boatload of prostrations and then they found some bells to ring and mantra wheels to turn. Finally, Dayita was done with the whole ordeal. I was at once shocked and a little disappointed in Dayita's excessive superstition. Despite her advanced level of understanding, there was a contrasting dimension to Dayita that bordered on silly, inane ideals. It was in large part due to her Buddhist upbringing, not all that different from some Christians unable to believe in anything other than Jesus, even if they necessarily do not fully believe in Jesus. More plainly, it was like a child finding it difficult to let go of the make-believe ideal of Santa Claus. Admittedly, I had placed her on a higher pedestal of understanding, only to find that she bought into the whole organization that seemed to be teeming with frauds, impostors, poseurs, and manipulators.

I told the *rinpoche* we had to go and he told Dayita to call him. I was just so glad to get away from the obnoxious bastard that I didn't care what he told Dayita.

The next morning at around eight, the phone rang.

"Hello?"

"Is Dayita there?"

Half asleep, I told Dayita that there was a call for her. I was too dazed to make anything out of it.

"Just hang up," she advised in an annoyed tone.

Clearly she knew exactly who it was. I hung up and a couple minutes later again the same guy calling. It was the young *rinpoche*. She spoke to him and told him off. He had apparently been in town and wanted to hang out with Dayita.

*How much nerve could you have to call my room and ask for my girlfriend?*

This guy just didn't know where to draw the line, but again I let it go.

Later that morning, we went to Boddha, about twenty minutes from Kathmandu, to check out some statues and as we arrived at the shop, the young *rinpoche* was there. Boddha was like many other Nepal towns with dusty alleys, round-the-clock traffic, motorcycles, dirt bikes, and air clogged with diesel exhaust. Again, he went on and on in Tibetan, and Dayita told him about how embarrassed she was by his actions. The guy just didn't get it. He did not care and said he wanted to make sure that she was okay.

I subsequently realized that he had found out my number when he asked me what hotel I was staying at. So again, he tried to find out where we were going today and I lied to him about our plans.

∼

I was stymied once again by the dismal appeal of Kathmandu, which apparently had no street cleaning as everyone threw trash in the streets and burned it in order to dispose of it.

Thinking I would feel a little better, I went to the casino to gamble a bit. Needless to say, I lost my money there. It felt as if the world was stacked irreversibly against me. My motivation and my excitement to go home had faded. I was in an indifferent state, transitioning to hopeless depression.

"What's wrong, Dar? It seems like you're dazed," Dayita asked me at lunch the next day.

"I'm not here anymore. My mind has checked out."

"I know. I can tell. It makes me sad."

We stared out the window at the bustling cars, all honking constantly and trying to get ahead and maneuver through the chaotic traffic. The mentality here was war, and it didn't help that this was my last stop at the end of a journey that wore me out completely. I had tired of living out of a backpack, trying endlessly to comprehend and to see through the morass of idiosyncratic cultural and social behaviors encountered in each nation. While there were moments of perfect euphoria, there also were plenty of other moments when the hardness of material reality eclipsed the potential for genuine spiritual bliss.

I had grown tired of all the differences, tangible and not so tangible. Differences like the lack of electricity, no warm water, bumpy and dusty roads, and the lack of a fixed price for anything, to name a few, made me miss America in unexpected ways. I couldn't speak any of the local languages, and, above all, there was the nagging feeling of being an outsider like a weight constantly pushing me down. Always somewhat proud of my ability to be patient, I had discovered with eye-opening frequency just how quickly I could lose that patience.

I wanted to hop on a plane immediately for San Francisco, but the thought of ending such a long journey on a low note and coming home because of weakness rather than strength was unbearable. The problems were surmountable so the decision to stay and make the trek to the formidable Everest base camp was actually easy to make.

~

# PART SIX

*Everest: Roots of Gratitude*

~

## 37

Mount Everest is the tallest mountain in the world, at 29,029 feet. Though few people try to brave the deadly hike all the way to the top in the month of May, when conditions are optimal, making the seven-day trek to base camp is a less life-threatening task. Base camp, at 17,700 feet, is set up by those groups who plan to make the trek to the top as a base for supplies, rest, acclimitization, and a dispatch location for emergencies, as there is a helicopter pad there.

I woke up sweating, heart racing thinking about the trek ahead. Anxiety gagged me and I ran to the toilet to puke. Never had I felt so nervous about realizing a goal that was so close to completion.

My mental fatigue amplified the now completely familiar feelings of separation and isolation. Dayita had returned to India the day before. Literally speaking, home was on the other side of the most imposing mountain on this planet. For me, utter terror now eclipsed this world.

My mind still was conditioned to certain luxuries—family, friends, warm beds, decent food, running water. My mind always won the race to settle itself in any of the places I had visited. I was like a tree staying long enough to set some roots down—some growing even as quickly a few inches per hour. However, each time I moved on, I was rudely uprooted, for better or worse.

My wakeup call rang so loudly by my ears that my heart raced anew and I ran again to the bathroom. Ready to make my long-awaited climb to the top of the world, I was battling an upset stomach that seemed intent on defying my objective. Breakfast arrived and I had planned a big meal the night before: eggs, hash browns, cereal, and bread and jam. Now, I couldn't touch even the bread. With each step, my nausea percolated but I struggled to resist the acid reflux that was churning through my esophagus. I rolled into a cab and headed to meet the guide.

*Okay, I don't feel so bad.*

As soon as I got out of the cab, I looked for a place to puke but the feeling subsided. I found another cab and headed to the airport. I wished Dayita hadn't left me. I met with my guide and couldn't manage more than a hello, despite his enthusiasm. We arrived at the airport, but this time, even after walking for a few feet, I was looking to puke. Perhaps I was going to die.

At the airport, I ran into the bathroom a few times, trying to force myself to throw up, but I was empty. Fifteen minutes after our scheduled departure, we boarded a bus with ten passengers who were going to fly on a two-propeller plane. Unexpectedly, though, our trip was aborted and we returned to the airport.

"The airport is now closed," the bus driver announced.

"Why? Who's here?" a passenger asked.

"The prime minister of Pakistan."

Apparently, he had also stayed at my hotel. I was convinced he was following me. There was red carpet laid out in the airport, hundreds of soldiers acting as security—all the pomp of a state visit. Unimpressed, I slept for an hour before making the trip back to the prop plane.

My guide and I hopped on a bus that took us past an enormous 747 plane marked by a Pakistani flag on its tail, which I assumed was for the use of the prime minister. Instead, we came up to a tiny twin propeller plane that clearly had been reused hundreds of times since the 1980s. They opened the side hatch door and we crawled into the cramped cabin that barely held all ten passengers. Not so lucky, I sat in the back, further amplifying the suffocating sense of claustrophobia that descended on me. Each of us was provisioned cotton balls for our ears. I didn't know if I should hold my ears, pucker up my butthole, or reach for the barf bag. The plane seemed barely sturdy, bouncing aimlessly like a feather caught in a gust that gyrated up and down at unpredictable speed. After about fifteen minutes, we were surrounded by the smallest of the Himalayan peaks. My heart dropped as I imagined we were heading straight to the center of those gargantuan tops. Suddenly, I could see through the front that the plane was diving sharply into a mountainside. Luckily, I didn't know at the time that this airport where we would be landing was considered, hands down, the world's most dangerous. I tensed up, thinking we would run headfirst into the invisible runway. To my surprise and relief, we landed smoothly on the steeply inclined runway that was much easier to land on than to take off from, mainly because of the drop at the end of the runway which, was at best guess more than a few thousand feet.

Behind the fence that marked the landing strip, I spotted more than twenty peasant villagers waiting to provide porter services. On the other side of the fence was a policeman with a rifle. We picked up our bags and immediately were on our way. Quite efficient, our guide already had a porter waiting for us.

At 11:00 AM, we went into a restaurant for lunch. Originally we were scheduled to start at 8:30 AM, and the delay had ratcheted my anxiety levels significantly. I forced down a third of my noodle soup and met my porter, a man with ragged jeans and sandals. He was planning on coming all the way up. He looked at my bag, asking the guide in Nepalese if that was all he had to carry. He seemed ecstatic that he only had to carry about fifty pounds uphill. The professional porters carried up to two hundred fifty pounds on their backs in less time than trekkers with nothing to carry and earned only the equivalent of eight dollars per day.

Shortly after we began walking, the effects of the thinner air impacted me. Thinking about Dayita seemed to fortify my motivation though, and I felt invigorated as we passed dozens of groups, ranging from five to more than twenty people speaking languages from all over the world, overtaking them. I looked back to find the guide and porter struggling to keep up with me. I had gone through a rather extensive time not doing any exercise and I was surprised at how well I was managing the rigors of the trek. I forgot all my worries and problems. After two more hours, we stopped at our endpoint for the day.

I ate a simple chicken broth soup, and still felt good so I urged my guide to let us continue. We trekked for another couple of hours through canyons, across suspended bridges over rivers, in the shade, in the sun, and even in the fog. It seemed like we went through every possible microclimate setting. The eagles soared overhead, leading the way and urging us forward. The air was as pure as Kathmandu's air was polluted—so crisp that it had the sensation of a clean drink of the fresh water. If my stomach had not been so upset, I would have said we were in heaven. As we studied the trail map, the entire journey seemed like it wouldn't be so bad after all—just a hop and a skip and I'd be at the top. Unfortunately, I did not have the experience to know otherwise. We accomplished three-quarters of the distance we needed to cover in two days. The progress exhilarated me and I even managed to catch up on emails—thanks to high altitude Wi-Fi service that I had not considered possible. I thought I would be out of civilization in the mountains but unlike Kathmandu, there were far more signs of civilization: less pollution, no trash littering the paths, and no vendors to harass me. Approaching the top of the world, the people didn't want to screw me.

Yet the isolation returned with a vengeance because I had no one to talk to. I sat on the uncomfortable wooden benches as it grew dark until I could no longer see the river coursing three hundred feet below. I waited silently as darkness and anxiety encroached upon every chamber and organ inside me. I decided to go to sleep early. It was 8:30 PM and we had ended the day at 2,800 meters. I walked down the stairs, came up to the small bright blue wooden door, unlocked the door, and entered. Finding the corner claustrophobic unit, I unfolded my sleeping bag and passed out for the night. Despite its claustrophobia, I was impressed with the accommodation's more-than-modest appearance— wood-built lodges with restaurants, a decent bed, and a personal toilet.

On the second day of the trek, I awoke to sharp knocks on neighbors' doors. Apparently, tea was being served at 5:30 AM. Not eager to participate in any early morning idiocy, I decided to sleep for another two hours. Of course, I awoke to see everybody preparing to leave.

I hustled quickly to get ready so we could leave at 8:00 AM and beat the group that had awakened me at 5:30 AM.

"You think we can beat the 5:30 AM group?" I asked my guide, referring to the gaggle of Germans who woke me up earlier that morning to pass around tea. The group comprised couples who were mostly middle aged— although there were a few who looked to be in their sixties or seventies. They seemed so well prepared with their new gear that I had settled on a personal mission to overtake them.

"Easy."

Sure enough, within forty minutes we caught them resting and easily overtook them. I had zeroed in on this goal of reaching the mountaintop as quickly as possible. The trek was now more scenic, with towering snow-capped peaks showing their faces. We earned our first look at Mount Everest, which, despite still being well off in the distance, at least fifty miles away, shook my core. My heart jumped, my body froze, and my eyes were transfixed.

*This is God! This is God! I'm seeing God.*

My whole being was in agreement. The energy of this peak, even at this distance, was as moving as I would have imagined an encounter with God Himself. I was compelled to bow as a Christian would facing his savior, a devout Muslim witnessing Mecca, or a Hindi meditating in the temple of Shiva. I am not religious, but there was something undeniable in this view.

This day's trek was not easy as the previous day. We started off at a good speed up the footpaths nestled on the edges of the mountainside, winding up around three hundred feet above the river and then coming back down to the river and crossing the suspended bridge. The path led us down to the riverbank and we started the slow climb that would eventually take us out of the river's sight for good. We crossed our final bridge, about one hundred feet above the river, trying not to look down. The hardest part of our hike was only beginning. We hit a zigzag trail of rocky steps and steep inclines with the roads twisting and turning so one could never see where they ended. At each turn, a new set of stairs awaited. After at least twenty-five times of turning what I thought was a definitive corner—hoping that there wouldn't be another uphill battle—we finally leveled out and were within the visible distance of our final stop for the day: Namche Bazar. We had gained altitude rapidly within a couple of hours.

Three hours later, we arrived at Namche Bazar, the biggest village on the trek, which contained plenty of shops, some specifically for the Everest climbers, who came down here when their gear failed. The village had Internet, Skype, fast computers, and every 21st century amenity one could request. It was like one never left Kathmandu—of course, minus the roaming yaks, porters toting heavy baskets twice their size, and chickens, donkeys, horses, and other members of a menagerie.

At the end of the day, I decided to take my first shower of the trek. The inn where we were staying had warmed water for me to bathe in and, afterward, the young Nepalese cook led me around the corner to an outdoor shack. With my thin, highly absorbent towel in hand, along with small shampoo containers from my hotel in Kathmandu, I hesitated before stripping naked, feeling my body tense up as I watched all of my body heat escape into the cold night air. With goosebumps all over my body, I ducked under the showerhead and turned the heat knob to full blast. As the warm water dripped down my hair, I ran my hand through my head and could only feel a matted mass of what used to be called hair. I immediately forgot how disgusted I was when the water went from defrosting warm to freezing cold without warning.

Screaming, I hopped out of the shower and wrapped my paper-thin towel around me. My body temperature now felt at least fifteen degrees colder and still half wet, and I put my clothes back on my shivering torso. Clumsily, I hopped on one foot with my shoe half on, trying not to touch my other foot on the wet ground while sliding my sock back on my still-soaked foot. The wind blew through the shack as if on some sadistic cue sending shivers down my spine and chilling every bone in my body. I ran out and back into my room, deciding this would be my last attempt at a shower until I returned to Kathmandu.

## 38

On the fifth day, I woke up feeling great—finally. I was ready to move on. The doctor gave me more antacid and sent me on my way. I put in my iPod, skipped to Cuban conga, and began ecstatically dancing on the trail, knowing I was now only a few stops away from my final destination. The clear blue sky lifted my spirits higher than the altitude of whose effects I had finally overcome. We passed the final wooden shacks of Namche Bazar as we climbed up the stairs through the village and past the last of the chickens who bid us farewell with their clucking cacophony. The topography for this part was mostly flat but I had my first stunning view of the ranges: Lhotse, Everest, and Ama Dablam. They were gorgeous monsters that simultaneously humbled and left me in awe. I had never bowed to anyone or anything willingly, but in the presence of these peaks I couldn't help but submit to their grandeur. The music blasting, I began dancing and skipping on a trail nestled in the side of a mountain. Staring at these peaks was like being in a rave hosted by nature. The euphoria was unsurpassed—until we hit the uphill section of the trek.

The riverbed was empty and the rhododendrons gave their own show. We passed the big group that stayed in our lodge on the first day, despite being a day behind schedule. I dropped my head and blazed my way through the trail; before I knew it we overtook the locals and their yaks that steadfastly headed uphill without the slightest concern for the ninety-degree heat. I gained some unique insight at this high-altitude scene. I realized that looking up only served as a form of discouragement, whereas looking straight down in front, focusing on every step, one by one, rather than thinking about the destination, allowed my legs to lift with magical strength. I was walking one step at a time, in my own world, before stopping in the thick of the forest and noticing that my guide was nowhere to be seen. I knew he wasn't in front of me but I couldn't believe that he wasn't right on my tail. I waited several minutes before he showed up, huffing and puffing. He had been struggling to keep up with me and, at this point, I realized the full power of being in the moment rather than wanting to be somewhere in the future more intuitively than ever before.

When I suggested a break, my guide was more than relieved. We had made the five-hour trek in three and a half hours, but upon arrival I started to feel anxiety and loneliness again—anxiety about being alone, anxiety about feeling sick in this remote part of the world, and anxiety about being so close to a goal. The room for my lodging was no bigger than a closet, the brown wood seeming darker than the clouds that engulfed our lodge. There was nothing left to do for the rest of the day. I tried to sleep, read, and listen to music, but it didn't help.

Luckily, my upset stomach had subsided but it was replaced by a terrible feeling of wanting to be somewhere so badly that it made me sick and scared that I might never get there. It felt like trying to avoid death. All my euphoria was replaced with its opposite.

## 39

The next couple of days were marked only by thinner levels of oxygen and the end of the tree line. The trek grew more taxing with every step into higher altitudes. There were no longer rhododendrons—only rocks and dirt. But above us towered beautiful peaks such as Alma Dablam that commanded our attention. The journey became simultaneously bleaker and more captivating.

On a break before a steep ascent into the higher realms of the Himalayas, breaking the 4,000-meter mark, we sat at an outdoor "café" to refuel. I ordered my pasta and stared observantly at an elderly woman who appeared to be in her late seventies. I watched as her guide helped her with her jacket and then her backpack. Once ready, she grabbed her walking stick and eyeshades and faced the upcoming ascent with the determination of a lion about to conquer her prey. Inspired, I recounted an earlier conversation with my father.

"Dad, you should really come to Everest with me. Do you realize what an epic journey it will be?"

"Daria, you know it is not good for me, at least not with my heart condition. The journey is tough and not meant for the elderly. Enjoy it while you can."

My father is just sixty.

Then I thought about myself and my personal will the previous night. I had slept miserably, unable to fully relax because as my breath drew deeper in my sleep, the oxygen was insufficient to sustain me. I woke up, gasping for air, as if I was being held under water. I spent the entire night thinking about the trek that was only going to get harder, wondering if I would really be able to complete it. With growing doubt and anxiety, I wondered whether I would end up heading back to Kathmandu on my own two feet or in a helicopter.

As I mused over the possible outcomes, my curiosity forbade me from speaking to this elderly woman who epitomized sheer will, embodied time-resistant strength, and conveyed a full essence of self-assurance in the face of all the adversity that nature could muster. She stood, unmoved by the fact that her presence was an inspirational miracle, at least to me. Casually, I approached her and told her the most looming thought in my mind. I'm sure it was on the minds of many at that café.

"You are a true inspiration to me," I told her with the most genuine tone possible.

"Thank you," she replied in the gentlest voice.

"At my age, I'm looking up at this trek, wondering if I'm going to make it, unsure about whether I have the will to do this. I honestly didn't know if I can do the next leg. You have given me a newfound strength to continue. How old are you, if you don't mind me asking?"

"I'm seventy-six."

"Your fearlessness is something I wish that every person had, especially myself."

"You know, I've been battling cancer for six years. It is not always easy, but you can't let anything get in the way of you living your life. You have to do whatever you want to do, no matter what your age or predicament."

I was blown away. The story was more moving than I had anticipated. At that point, all my fears dissipated and I wished—truly wished—that every person would be blessed with such courage. One need not look to moguls, business professionals, celebrities, or even great athletes for encouragement. Sometimes, the biggest miracles lay right in front of our vision. Listening and seeing are all we really need.

I climbed for the next hour, up the steep ascent that, at times, was more akin to rock climbing. I witnessed the locals carrying lumber—several ten-foot-high two-by-fours—towering over them along the same path. I could only imagine how grueling their journey must have been. Granted, they were probably more accustomed to the little oxygen there was up here, but they made up for it by carrying several hundred pounds uphill, and all this in the hopes of making enough money to provide for themselves and their younger siblings.

We edged over a final hump and came upon the epic mountains: Nuptse, Lhotse, Everest, and several other notable peaks. I was now in the realm of wonders, captivated by the peaks that scraped the heavens.

The ground began to shake me out of my daydream. I was brought back to the reality that this was not heaven. There was a roaring sound of thunder but not a cloud in the sky to account for it. I looked around, nervous that an earthquake was occurring. I looked to my guide.

"What was that?"

"That was an avalanche on Nuptse," he said, pointing straight across.

*These things really are monsters. They look like monsters, feel like monsters, and sound like monsters.*

The grandeur was supremely terrifying.

We continued onto our final lodge at 5,200 meters, with effects of inadequate sleep and altitude sickness working their symptoms with more severe impact. One symptom was not being able to breathe deeply. Another was that every step I took became twice as tiring as the previous one. My endurance was being sapped with every meter I gained in altitude. The weather conditions did their own magic as our lodge barely protected against the elements, mainly because insulation was nonexistent. Wrapped in layers of undershirts, a fleece jacket, a down jacket, and my down sleeping bag, I lay there, shivering futilely for warmth.

This was to be our most difficult day. Our agenda involved trekking up to the next cabin, checking in, and then continuing to base camp and then returning to the cabin. While every day to this point had been a three- to five-hour day of trekking, this was to be a seven- to eight-hour day, with the effects of altitude sickness and sleeplessness that much more pronounced.

After finishing lunch at the final cabin, we headed towards base camp, which I spotted as soon as we reared our heads over the hill. The issue with being surrounded by such large mountains was that everything was deceivingly close—much like my visit to Las Vegas, when I thought it would be prudent to walk from the Bellagio to the Venetian.

*It's just right there—across the street and a couple hotels down!*

Little did I know that just across the street and a couple of hotels down meant at least a mile. Similarly, the Everest base camp was just down the hill and a little further ahead. In reality, it was at least a couple of miles away, and what I thought would be a twenty-minute hike turned out to be closer to two hours. I passed beautiful vibrant aqua blue glaciers, with rocks strewn aside the frozen mass of water.

Out of breath and ready to call it a day, I finally arrived at base camp.

"Smile!" said a couple I met at lunch as they snapped photos of me.

I barely managed a smile, looking around for an oxygen tank. All around dozens of tents were pitched, adorned with large banners boasting their accomplishments.

*John Superaccomplished has climbed six of the tallest peaks in just fifty days!*

Shit! At this point, making it to base camp of one mountain was the best accomplishment I could have hoped for.

Beyond me stood the overpass to Everest, and, in between that overpass and me, ice sheets with fifty-foot gaps between them. Gaps of death imposed their awesome risks—they probably dug to the center of the earth, as far as I was concerned. To me, the scene looked like the thorny forest that the prince had to fight through in order to get to the Sleeping Beauty. Rocks sat on sheets of ice. One would think that the ground consisted of rock, but here we stood on ice. Snow began falling, some of it landing in my eyes as I gazed at these natural skyscrapers that would make any human attempt at matching their size a laughable endeavor. I shrank immediately in comparison.

Before I could take it all in (and I wasn't sure that even if I spent days here I could truly take it all in), we had to head back before dark. I spotted a helicopter in the distance drawing nearer as a group headed to the landing pad, holding one man in their arms. The helicopter landed, quickly swooping up the man, who had to be escorted back for whatever reason. All his dreams and aspirations of climbing Everest had ended. This added an ominous dimension to our return to the lodge.

Halfway back, I sat on a rock to catch my breath.

"Don't sit here," my guide told me.

"Why not?"

"Rocks fall up there. Last week one woman died," he told me, pointing to the loose boulders.

That was reason enough to immediately jump and continue. I returned to our cabin around four in the afternoon, completely exhausted.

"Tomorrow morning, we wake at 4:45 AM for Kala Pathar," my guide said.

As if the day wasn't hard enough, I had yet another leg to Kala Pathar, where one could catch the best views of Everest. And with this in mind, I headed to bed around 7:00 PM, in the naïve hope of catching up on sleep. Two unsuccessful hours later, I returned to the main room to find that I wasn't alone. No one could sleep. Eyes red, coughs abundant, everyone smelling like yaks—we all sat there in misery. The old adage that "misery enjoys company" could be summed up in an image of our group sitting there, waiting for daylight.

"Wake up, Daria."

I heard my guide knocking on my door.

I was hoping it was a bad dream because I had finally just fallen asleep. This was it—the final push uphill for breathtaking views; it would be downhill from there, literally.

I struggled out of bed and from the looks of the empty common room, we were the first ones out the door. My enthusiasm at being so close to our goal helped propel me uphill. The grade on this final bit was three times higher, as if we were going up a set of stairs. The trail didn't seem to end because looking upward, it disappeared into the clouds.

"Are we even going to be able to see Everest with these clouds?" I asked.

"Maybe. We see, sometime clouds open if we lucky," the guide said in the most routine way possible.

Whether I saw Everest or not, I was determined to make my objective. Two hours later, we were within striking distance of the top, but now it was snowing and boulders impeded our way. Here, it became tricky. I was reminded of Nickelodeon's Aggro Crag from the show *Guts*. Thee kids had to climb artificial boulders in spite of confetti falling in their faces in order to reach the top of the "Crag." This was now my task, in this remote part of the Himalayas—except I faced real boulders and snow.

We cleverly navigated our way through and around the boulders, finally reaching the top. I half expected to see a button waiting to be pushed at the top, signaling that I was the first to reach it. Not only did the snow prevent us from catching a glimpse of Everest, but I could barely see my hand in front of my face. It was becoming dangerous as every angle view of the top had a steep drop other than the side we climbed. One wrong move and I'd be on a long deathly tumble. I stood, rejoicing in my final accomplishment for another fifteen minutes, and then the Forrest Gump syndrome took hold of me. I just wanted to run. Only I knew where I was going: home.

With every step toward the lower altitude, I felt stronger, fresher, and more enthusiastic. I began to run, paying no heed to whether my guide would be able to keep up. We started our descent from Kala Pathar at 7:00 AM and by the time we ended at 4:00 PM, we had covered the equivalent of what would have been a three-day journey on our way up the promontory. Though we had lost a couple days to my upset stomach at Namche Bazar, we more than made up for it on our descent. At my rate, not only would we not be a day behind, but we would finish a day early.

It took us two days to return to our "base camp" which was the town we would wait in before our flight back to Kathmandu. My excitement unleashed, I managed fantastic sleep and the air was as full of oxygen as I'd ever breathed it.

≈

I awoke the final morning to catch my 6:00 AM flight to Kathmandu. I packed my bag, ready as ever to start the long journey back home. In the airport, I found all the friends I had made along the way who also were getting ready for their flights.

"Flight 504," a voice from the intercom bleated as passengers headed onto the tarmac to board their prop plane.

I watched on in envy, anxious to board my impending flight.

"When is our flight?" I asked the guide.

"We will be two flights after this," he said with a reassuring tone.

Ten minutes later, the next flight left, rolling down the steep landing strip that ended in a thousand-foot drop. I felt nervous as I watched the clouds roll into the scene.

"Flight 506 has been delayed," the voice from the intercom intoned.

Sadly, I went to the bakery, looking through my wallet to see how much money I had left. There was barely enough to buy another pastry. Hopefully, my guide would have enough to spare me if my flight was canceled.

The clouds turned to rain and I watched as my chances of leaving disappeared with the showers. I got wind that there would be a prioritizing of passengers due to the fact that several dozen people didn't get to leave that day. It was only 7:00 AM and we were forced to wait until 3:00 PM for the planes to determine their passenger order for the following day. I couldn't afford to miss, as my flight home was the following day.

"Listen, you have to tell them that I have an international flight that I cannot miss. I have to be on the first plane out of here."

My guide nodded, understanding my predicament.

"Don't worry. Owner of lodge knows plane people and can make you go first."

I rested, assured as I watched everyone battle for position as soon as the airplane company's doors opened. It was warfare and despite being reassured by my guide, I made my way to the front to explain my situation to the staff. They paid close attention to what I had to say when I explained that if I didn't leave tomorrow, I'd miss an international flight to the U.S. Within an hour my position was determined and I was to be on the second flight out the following morning.

Having put that worry behind me, I scrounged in my pockets to see what I had left. A mere two dollars were all that emerged. I looked around and found the only store where my money would be able to buy something: the candy store. Well, it wasn't a candy store, but they did carry Smarties. They came in all different colors in a cylindrical plastic case. I bought three for seventy-five cents and left the store. As I walked out, I saw three kids, about four years old, sitting in their torn sweatpants and wrapped up in a jacket, no doubt a hand-me-down from their elder siblings. As I approached the group, their heads all tilted upward, looking at me, a foreigner, in complete confusion. I kneeled and looked at them intently.

"Here," I said, handing over all three packs.

Their expressions were a complete surprise. They did not believe that such a thing was possible and they burst out in hysterical yet joyful laughter. They yelled urgently for their fourth friend to come, as if he was missing his ticket to paradise. The fourth boy was completely clueless as to what was happening but as soon as they showed him the candy, he understood completely. I still had a little change left over, so I went back to the store and bought another one for this boy. They sat ecstatically on the curb, laughing, screaming, and sharing their candy.

The simplicity of it all floored me. One would have thought that I was leading an armada of black Land Cruisers, carrying supplies to provision them. At least, for a brief moment, I was the alien who took them to paradise, even if just for the shortest possible trip.

~

I survived the peaks of Everest, the grueling trek to base camp, and the most dangerous airport in the whole world and made it back to Kathmandu. It was now time to finally head home. I packed my bags. I sat in the airport, reflecting on the whole experience. I had traveled far and wide for a new perspective. All my life I had possessed the essential tools to find inner happiness, but I had lacked the fundamental ability to allow myself to be happy because I always looked for the predictable outward signs.

Only now I was blessed with the ability to visualize the roots of gratitude that were surprisingly inside me, waiting for me to swap out the ego-driven forces for a fully enriched sense of humility. It is that humility that allows us to accept the stark realization that this life is out of our control and whatever we have, we must cherish, as nothing will last forever.

A part of me never returned on that flight back to the U.S. It will forever keep its heart in the majestic mountains of the Himalayas, the tranquil jungles of southern India, the peaceful steppes of the Mongolian countryside, and the heartwarming sunsets of Bali. And while there is a part of me that died on that trip as a result of my new-found perspective on the essence of being, I still continue on, living life in the West as one would be expected to—with material ambitions and material goals for the future.

However, there is one small difference: I'm not actually here. And I will never be back.

As I fell into the warm loving embrace of my mother, father, and brother, I was finally home, and though I rested easy in that fact, something deep inside me discomfited me. It was the voice telling me that no one would ever fully know who I have become.

# Epilogue

Even now as I continue to process and make sense of my long journey, I continue to believe even more strongly that much of our disappointment comes from lack of clarity about what we want absent of our consumer needs. Which element comes first? Clarity? Determination?

Conceivably, one can have no determination without clarity—it's much like having strong legs with no eyes. It is only with clarity that the reserves of every soulful force and source of perceptive power embedded within ourselves come to light. Like essential vitamins and nutrients, courage and determination are absorbed from an endless source as powerful as the sun, and they are manifested in their natural forms if we permit them to appear. Only then is the nourishment capable of enlivening the colorful palette our lives take on, not just in our imaginations, but in the ways in which we respond to the sensory impulses triggered by our imaginations.

Obviously, I have not forsaken the trappings of a well-heeled life in the Bay Area, but I can count on the external and internal renewals of energy always coming when I need them the most. They can be in the form of a person, dream, nature—or even an internal shift of perception that manifests itself practically without me being necessarily aware of it at the outset.

The next question: What is reality? Is it outside in the things we see?

I'm convinced that it's not. Prior to my journey, my home and my interaction with everything around me starkly differed from what I encountered when I returned ten months later. What changed? Externally, nothing. I still live in the same house and see the same people, but internally, everything has changed.

Evolution is an innate process representing who we are, and if we accept the firm, hopeful conclusion that everything will be just fine, then how can we take advantage of hardship, which really is opportunity in disguise? If we are afraid, if we hesitate, or if we are skeptical because of what we don't fully know or understand, hardship offers the chance to be courageous. If we see death, we learn to cherish life; if we are annoyed, we challenge ourselves to be patient. It is perfectly acceptable to have and to acknowledge negative feelings, but we must be willing to bear them with the perspective that those feelings will not drag us to the point of utter paralysis or numbness. The outside world will not change but our individual reaction, perspective, interaction, and understanding can.

I'm sure you've heard the line: You can only hear what you are ready to hear. Deceivingly simple, but it can be frighteningly complicated. It can be shocking to look within and be wholly terrified by what is seen. That is okay. Take what you are ready to digest and don't bite off more than you can chew. Trust me, the mind is a faithful enough companion to let you know the right amount at the right time and at the right place.

Regardless of our upbringing, status, and roots, the life game offers the same set of rules. Pretty simple: with life there is death, we have essential needs to survive, and so on. However, very few of us choose to participate fully in this game. Like weekend warriors or armchair enthusiasts, we can be easily soothed by just sitting on the sidelines, preferring instead to be envious—if not intensely jealous—of those who get into the game, bruises and all. The greatest gift I've experienced is escaping the taint of life-hindering inhibition. Dance if you want to dance, strike up a conversation with the stranger next to you, do what you want without thinking, worrying, or fearing something, especially if it involves criticism from others who sit on the sidelines and secretly are jealous of your ability to live with no reservations or apologies—without, of course, causing unjustifiable harm or pain to others around you.

What do we truly seek? If money is what you want, go after it, indulge in it, and let it take you over until you are ready to evolve through your experience. I guess I was lucky enough to have an epiphany early on—on my twenty-second birthday. Asked to make a wish, I understood that I had every external thing I could want: a loving family, beautiful girlfriend, my dream car, a perfect setup with the family business, and an endless list of friends, relatives, acquaintances, and objects. The only thing I missed was the capacity to have and express gratitude for all of this. Without gratitude, I suddenly realized that this whole heap of personal and material riches would be a tragic waste. So, again, what do we seek? I set out expecting to look for happiness, not realizing that happiness is a flower whose roots are in gratitude. Put simply, a billionaire without gratitude is a poor man and a poor man with gratitude is a wealthy man. I mean true gratitude: the feeling of an all-encompassing love for everything, not just in the tangents of the five senses but also within every imaginable plane our mind explores and occupies. True love and compassion can only stem from gratitude.

Now I understand why gratitude is so ubiquitous. Life's greatest satisfaction comes from knowing its beautiful paradox or exquisite anarchy, explainable only by a keen sense of gratitude. Far away from the familiar comforts of the Bay Area, I realized that my life began many thousands of miles away at the absolute frontier end of my comfort zone. In the starkest moments of my greatest discomfort I realized why death truly transmits the greatest meaning to our life.

# About the Author

 Daria grew up in Tiburon, CA where he attended private high school. By the age of 20, having graduated from the University of Southern California in just three years, he took over his father's company. After a year of successful work, he realized that the rat race was not his passion and sought to learn more about himself and his true interests. As a teenager, Daria felt a keen interest in the deeper questions in life and aspired to learn the essence of Buddhism. At the age of 22, he set out on an adventure that forever changed his life. He learned from experts in their respective fields about Aikido, yoga, and Buddhism. Authorities such as 8th dan instructor Isoyama Shihan, who taught the world-renowned Steven Segal, imparted their knowledge of the truth of Aikido to Daria. Furthermore, Daria studied at the Sivananda ashram where the spirit and teachings of Sivananda, regarded as an authority on Vedanta yoga, remains. Finally, his meetings in Nepal were with one of the foremost monks of the Nyigma lineage, who personally imparted deep Buddhist truths to Daria. Truths that many spend years trying to grasp. Daria currently resides in Marin County, CA.

Made in the USA
San Bernardino, CA
09 December 2013